brilliant barbecues

Silverdale Books

Published in 2001 by Silverdale Books
An Imprint of Bookmart Ltd.
Registered Number 2372865
Trading as Bookmart Limited
Desford Road
Enderby
Leicester
LE9 5AD

Brilliant Barbecues
Designed & Compiled by: R&R Publications Marketing Pty. Ltd.
Creative Director: Paul Sims
Production Manager: Anthony Carroll
Food Photography: Warren Webb, William Meppem, Andrew Elton, Quentin Bacon, Gary Smith, Per Ericson, Paul Grater, Ray Joice, John Stewart, Ashley Mackevicius, Harm Mol, Yanto Noerianto, Andy Payne.
Food Stylists: Stephane Souvlis, Janet Lodge, Di Kirby, Wendy Berecry, Belinda Clayton, Rosemary De Santis, Carolyn Fienberg, Jacqui Hing, Michelle Gorry, Christine Sheppard, Donna Hay.
Recipe Development: Ellen Argyriou, Sheryle Eastwood, Kim Freedman, Lucy Kelly, Donna Hay, Anneka Mitchell, Penelope Peel, Jody Vassallo, Belinda Warn, Loukie Werle.
Proof Reader: Andrea Hazell-Tarttelin

Includes Index
ISBN 1 85605 650 3
EAN 9781856056502

First Edition Printed June 2001
Computer Typeset in Humanist 521 & Times New Roman

Printed in China

nts

introduction

Which barbecue?

There are many different barbecues available. The one you choose will depend on your budget, how many people you regularly feed and whether barbecuing is usually a planned or an impromptu affair.

Gas barbecues:

These barbecues contain lava rocks which are heated by gas burners. The lava rocks evenly distribute the heat and if you have a barbecue with multiple burners it is possible to have the rocks hot on one side and a medium heat on the other. The rack on which you cook the food is set above the rocks. Gas barbecues also require a gas bottle, which needs to be refilled on a regular basis – this is relatively inexpensive. When lighting a gas barbecue it is important to follow the manufacturer's instructions. If the barbecue does not ignite immediately, turn it off, wait for any build up of gas to disperse, then try again.

Wood or coal barbecues:

The key to using these types of barbecues is patience and planning. These barbecues take up to an hour to heat, so you need to remember to light the barbecue well in advance.

Electric barbecues:

These are ideal for people who want to barbecue indoors and, like gas barbecues, they produce almost instant heat.

How hot?

The recipes in this book were cooked on a gas barbecue. Gas barbecues heat up very quickly and the heat is relatively easy to control, however if your barbecue uses coal, wood or barbecue fuel, you need to allow 30-45 minutes for coals to heat and 45 minutes to 1 hour for wood. The following is a guide for assessing the heat of these barbecues.

Hot fire:

There will be a red glow showing through the thin layer of white ash and when you hold your hand 15 cm/6 in above the coals you will only be able to leave it there for 3 seconds. This fire is ideal for searing and quick cooking.

Medium fire:

The red glow will be almost gone and the ash thicker and more grey in colour. When you hold your hand 15 cm/6 in above the coals you will be able to leave it there for 5-7 seconds. Most barbecuing is done on this heat.

W

barbecue

Low fire:

The red glow will have disappeared and there will be a thick coating of grey ash. This heat is ideal for slow cooking of foods.

The amount of heat reaching the food on these barbecues can also be controlled by moving the rack closer to or further away from the fire.

If you have a wood barbecue, interesting flavours can be imparted to the food by using different types of wood. It is well to be aware that there are some plants that are poisonous and wood from those plants or chemically treated timber, is not suitable for barbecuing. Depending on where you live some of the following may be available: fruit woods, such as cherry and apple, which give a mild sweet flavour that is delicious when cooking pork, poultry and fish; grapevine cuttings – these give a delicate sweet flavour that is excellent for fish and poultry. Herbs such as rosemary and thyme also give interesting flavours when burned on the barbecue.

which
barbecue

Play it safe

As with any type of cooking, basic safety rules should always be observed. However with barbecuing there are a few extra that you need to remember.

- *If you have a gas barbecue, before lighting it check that all the gas fittings and hose connections are tight.*
- *If your gas barbecue does not light first time, turn it off, wait 20 seconds and try again. This will ensure that there is no gas build-up.*
- *Always turn a gas barbecue off at the gas bottle as well as at the controls.*
- *Check the barbecue area before lighting the barbecue. Do not have the barbecue too close to the house and sweep up any dry leaves or anything that might catch fire if hit by a spark.*
- *Watch a lighted barbecue at all times. Keep children and pets away from hot barbecues and equipment.*
- *Do not barbecue in enclosed areas. If wet weather has forced you to move your barbecue undercover, ensure there is plenty of ventilation.*
- *Remember always to check the manufacturer's safety instructions that come with your barbecue.*

Equipment check

Use this checklist to ensure that you have the basic equipment for successful barbecuing.

oven mitt or cloth – *important for handling hot skewers, racks and frying pans.*

tongs – *these should be long-handled so that you can turn food without burning your hands. Use tongs for turning food, testing to see if steak is done and moving coals and hot racks.*

basting brushes – *these are used to brush food with marinades, oil, butter or sauce during cooking.*

spatulas – *essential for turning delicate foods, such as fish, so that they do not fall apart. The best type has a long, wide blade and a long handle.*

selection of sharp knives – *use for preparation and carving cooked food.*

hinged grills, wire baskets – *these come in many shapes and sizes for cooking whole fish and other foods that are difficult to turn. Always oil the grill or basket before using so that the food does not stick.*

skewers – *bamboo or wooden skewers are good for quick cooking of foods. Before use, soak them in water to prevent them from burning during cooking. Before threading food onto bamboo or wooden skewers, lightly oil them so that the cooked food will slip off easily. Metal skewers are better for heavier foods.*

marinating pans and bowls – *remember that most marinades contain an acid ingredient so the best choice of dish for marinating is glass, ceramic, stainless steel or enamel. Deep-sided disposable aluminium dishes are also good for marinating.*

appetisers

Middle Eastern dip

appetisers

Whilst the barbecue is warming up

and to put your guests into a casual mood, serve a selection of off-barbecue appetisers with drinks. These tasty morsels will really get things going.

middle eastern dip

Photograph page 9

ingredients

1 large eggplant (aubergine)
1 onion, unpeeled
2 cloves garlic, crushed
olive oil
2 tablespoons lemon juice
2 tablespoons chopped fresh parsley
1/4 cup/60g/2oz sour cream
4 pieces lavash bread, cut into triangles

Method:

1 *Preheat barbecue to a high heat. Place eggplant (aubergine) and onion on lightly oiled barbecue grill and cook, turning occasionally, for 20-30 minutes or until skins of eggplant (aubergine) and onion are charred and flesh is soft. Cool slightly, peel and chop roughly.*

2 *Place eggplant (aubergine), onion, garlic, 1/4 cup/60mL/2fl oz oil and lemon juice in a food processor or blender and process until smooth. Add parsley and sour cream and mix to combine.*

3 *Brush bread lightly with oil and cook on barbecue for 1-2 minutes each side or until crisp. Serve immediately with dip.*

Lavash bread is a yeast-free Middle Eastern bread available from Middle Eastern food shops and some supermarkets. If unavailable use pitta bread instead.

Serves 6

spicy barbecued nuts

ingredients

250g/8oz honey roasted peanuts
185g/6oz pecans
125g/4 oz macadamia nuts
125g/4oz cashews
1 tablespoon sweet paprika
1 tablespoon ground cumin
2 teaspoons garam masala
1 teaspoon ground coriander
1 teaspoon ground nutmeg
1/4 teaspoon cayenne pepper or according to taste
1 tablespoon olive oil

Method:

1 *Preheat barbecue to a medium heat. Place peanuts, pecans, macadamia nuts and cashews in a bowl and mix to combine. Add paprika, cumin, garam masala, coriander, nutmeg and cayenne pepper and toss to coat.*

2 *Heat oil on barbecue plate (griddle), add nut mixture and cook, turning frequently, for 5 minutes or until nuts are golden. Cool slightly before serving.*

Warning: *the nuts are very hot when first removed from the barbecue and they retain their heat for quite a long time - so caution your guests when you serve these delicious nibbles.*

Serves 6

Oven temperature 180°C, 350°F, Gas 4

smoked salmon and watercress roulade

Method:

1 *Place watercress leaves, parsley, egg yolks, flour and pepper to taste in a food processor and process until mixture is smooth. Transfer watercress mixture to a bowl. Place egg whites in a bowl and beat until stiff peaks form. Fold egg white mixture into watercress mixture.*

2 *Spoon roulade mixture into a greased and lined 26x32cm/10 1/2x12 3/4 in Swiss roll tin and bake for 5 minutes or until just cooked. Turn roulade onto a damp teatowel and roll up from short side. Set aside to cool.*

3 *To make filling, place cream cheese, sour cream, smoked salmon and lemon juice in a food processor and process until mixture is smooth. Stir gelatine mixture into smoked salmon mixture.*

4 *Unroll cold roulade, spread with filling and reroll. Cover and chill. Cut into slices to serve.*

Serves 10

ingredients

1 bunch/90g/3oz watercress
1 teaspoon finely chopped fresh parsley
2 eggs, separated
2 tablespoons flour
freshly ground black pepper

Smoked salmon filling
60g/2oz cream cheese
2 tablespoons sour cream
90g/3oz smoked salmon
1 teaspoon lemon juice
1 1/2 teaspoons gelatine dissolved in
1 1/2 tablespoons hot water, cooled

fruit
and cheese platter

Photograph page 13

Method:

1 *Place lemon juice in a small bowl, add red and green apple wedges and toss to coat. This will help prevent the apple wedges from going brown.*

2 *Arrange red and green apple wedges, kiwifruit slices, orange segments, Camembert, Stilton and tasty (mature cheddar) cheeses attractively with biscuits and dip on a large platter.*

Note: *Choose fruit in season and arrange with your favourite cheeses on a large platter.*

Serves 10

ingredients

3 tablespoons fresh lemon juice
2 red-skinned apples, cored and cut into wedges
2 green-skinned apples, cored and cut into wedges
4 kiwifruit, peeled and cut into slices
2 oranges, peeled, segmented and white pith removed
100g/4oz Camembert cheese
100g/4oz Stilton cheese
100g/4oz tasty cheese (mature cheddar), choose your favourite brand
cheese biscuits, purchased or homemade

---

passion fruit
yoghurt dip

Photograph page 13

Method:

1 *Place yogurt, honey and passion fruit pulp in a bowl and mix to combine.*
The perfect accompaniment to any fresh fruit.

Makes 2 cups/400g/12½oz

ingredients

2 cups/400 g/12½oz unsweetened natural yogurt
2 tablespoons honey
3 tablespoons passion fruit pulp or pulp 4-5 passion fruit

guacamole
with tortillas

Photograph page 15

ingredients

6 corn tortillas

Chilli butter
90g/3oz butter
2 teaspoons finely grated lemon rind
2 teaspoons sweet chilli sauce
1 teaspoon ground cumin

Guacamole
1 avocado, halved, stoned and peeled
1 tomato, peeled and finely chopped
2 tablespoons lemon juice
1 tablespoon finely chopped fresh coriander or parsley

Method:

1. *To make Chilli Butter, place butter, lemon rind, chilli sauce and cumin in a bowl and mix to combine.*
2. *To make Guacamole, place avocado in a bowl and mash with a fork. Stir in tomato, lemon juice and coriander or parsley.*
3. *Place tortillas in a single layer on a baking tray and heat on barbecue for 3-5 minutes or until warm.*

To serve: *Place Chilli Butter, Guacamole and tortillas on a platter so that each person can spread a tortilla with Chilli Butter, top with Guacamole, then roll up and eat.*

Serves 6

---

cheese
and bacon nachos

Photograph page 15

Oven temperature 180°C, 350°F, Gas 4

ingredients

6 rashers bacon, finely chopped
6 spring onions, finely chopped
4 jalapeño chillies, finely chopped
200g/6½oz packet corn chips
125g/4oz grated tasty cheese (mature cheddar)
1 cup/250g/8oz sour cream

Method:

1. *Cook bacon, spring onions and chillies in a nonstick frying pan over a medium heat for 4-5 minutes or until crisp. Remove from pan and drain on absorbent kitchen paper.*
2. *Place corn chips in a shallow oven-proof dish and sprinkle with bacon mixture and cheese. Bake for 5-8 minutes or until heated through and cheese is melted. Serve immediately, accompanied with sour cream for dipping.*

Jalapeño chillies: *These are the medium-to-dark green chillies that taper to a blunt end and are 5-7½ cm/2-3 in long and 2-2½cm/¾-1 in wide. They are medium-to-hot in taste and are also available canned or bottled.*

Serves 6

whole fish
in banana leaves

Method:

1 *Preheat barbecue to a medium heat. Blanch banana leaf in boiling water for 1 minute, drain, pat dry and set aside.*

2 *To make stuffing, place rice, pistachio nuts, sun-dried peppers or tomatoes, spring onions, dill, lemon rind and garlic in a bowl and mix to combine. Spoon stuffing into cavity of fish and secure opening with wooden toothpicks or cocktail sticks.*

3 *Place fish in centre of banana leaf, top with lime slices and dill and fold banana leaf around fish to completely enclose. Secure with wooden toothpicks or cocktail sticks. Alternately wrap fish in lightly oiled aluminium foil.*

4 *Place fish on barbecue grill and cook for 7-10 minutes, turn and cook for 7-10 minutes longer or until flesh flakes when tested with a fork.*

Serves 4

ingredients

1 large banana leaf
1 large whole fish such as sea bass or snapper, cleaned and skin scored at 3cm/1 1/4in intervals
1 lime, thinly sliced
4 sprigs fresh dill

Nutty rice stuffing

1 cup/220g/7oz wild rice blend, cooked
90g/3oz pistachio nuts, chopped
3 tablespoons finely chopped sun-dried peppers or tomatoes
3 spring onions, chopped
1 tablespoon chopped fresh dill
1 teaspoon finely grated lemon rind
1 clove garlic, chopped

grilled
cod and potatoes

Photograph page 17

Method:

1 *Preheat barbecue to a medium heat. Place 1 tablespoon oil, lime juice and black peppercorns in a bowl and mix to combine. Brush oil mixture over fish and marinate at room temperature for 10 minutes.*

2 *Brush potatoes with oil and sprinkle with salt. Place potatoes on lightly oiled barbecue grill and cook for 5 minutes each side or until tender and golden. Move potatoes to side of barbecue to keep warm.*

3 *Place fish on lightly oiled barbecue grill and cook for 3-5 minutes each side or until flesh flakes when tested with a fork. To serve, arrange potatoes attractively on serving plates and top with fish.*

Serves

ingredients

3 tablespoons olive oil
2 tablespoons lime juice
1 teaspoon crushed black peppercorns
4 cod cutlets
6 potatoes, very thinly sliced
sea salt

hot chilli prawns (shrimp)

ingredients

1½kg/3 lb uncooked large prawns, (shrimp) peeled and deveined with tails left intact

Chilli marinade

2 teaspoons cracked black pepper
2 tablespoons sweet chilli sauce
1 tablespoon soy sauce
1 clove garlic, crushed
¼ cup/60 mL/2 fl oz lemon juice

Mango cream

1 mango, peeled, stoned and roughly chopped
3 tablespoons coconut milk

Method:

1. *To make marinade, place black pepper, chilli sauce, soy sauce, garlic and lemon juice in a bowl and mix to combine. Add prawns (shrimp), toss to coat, cover and set aside to marinate for 1 hour. Toss several times during marinating.*
2. *To make Mango Cream, place mango flesh and coconut milk in a food processor or blender and process until smooth.*
3. *Preheat barbecue to a medium heat. Drain prawns (shrimp) and cook on lightly oiled barbecue for 3-4 minutes or until prawns change colour. Serve immediately with Mango Cream.*

Coconut milk: *This can be purchased in a number of forms: canned, as a long-life product in cartons, or as a powder to which you add water. Once opened it has a short life and should be used within a day or so. It is available from Asian food stores and some supermarkets, however if you have trouble finding it you can easily make your own. To make coconut milk, place 500 g/1 lb desiccated coconut in a bowl and add 3 cups/750mL/1¼pt of boiling water. Set aside to stand for 30 minutes, then strain, squeezing the coconut to extract as much liquid as possible. This will make a thick coconut milk. The coconut can be used again to make a weaker coconut milk.*

Serves 6

salmon
cutlets with pineapple salsa

Method:

1. *Preheat barbecue to a medium heat. Cook salmon cutlets on lightly oiled barbecue for 3-5 minutes each side or until flesh flakes when tested with a fork.*
2. *To make salsa, place pineapple, spring onions, chilli, lemon juice and mint in a food processor or blender and process to combine. Serve at room temperature with salmon cutlets.*

Cook's tip: *If fresh pineapple is unavailable use a can of drained crushed pineapple in natural juice in its place.*

Note: *This salsa is delicious served with any fish or barbecued chicken.*

Serves 4

ingredients

4 salmon cutlets, cut 2½cm/1 in thick

Pineapple salsa
250g/8oz roughly chopped fresh pineapple
2 spring onions, finely chopped
1 fresh red chilli, seeded and finely chopped
1 tablespoon lemon juice
2 tablespoons finely chopped fresh mint

squid
and scallop salad

ingredients

1 red pepper, seeded and halved
1 yellow or green pepper, seeded and halved
2 squid (calamari) tubes
250g/8oz scallops, roe (coral) removed
250g/8oz asparagus, cut into 5cm/2in pieces, blanched
1 red onion, sliced
3 tablespoons fresh coriander leaves
1 bunch rocket or watercress

Herb and balsamic dressing
1 tablespoon finely grated fresh ginger
1 tablespoon chopped fresh rosemary
1 clove garlic, crushed
1/4 cup/60mL/2fl oz olive oil
2 tablespoons lime juice
1 tablespoon balsamic or red wine vinegar

Method:

1. *To make dressing, place ginger, rosemary, garlic, oil, lime juice and vinegar in a screwtop jar and shake well to combine. Set aside.*
2. *Preheat barbecue to a high heat. Place red and yellow or green pepper halves, skin side down on lightly oiled barbecue grill and cook for 5-10 minutes or until skins are blistered and charred. Place peppers in a plastic food bag or paper bag and set aside until cool enough to handle. Remove skins from peppers and cut flesh into thin strips.*
3. *Cut squid (calamari) tubes lengthwise and open out flat. Using a sharp knife cut parallel lines down the length of the squid (calamari), taking care not to cut through the flesh. Make more cuts in the opposite direction to form a diamond pattern. Cut into 5cm/2in squares.*
4. *Place squid (calamari) and scallops on lightly oiled barbecue plate (griddle) and cook, turning several times, for 3 minutes or until tender. Set aside to cool slightly.*
5. *Combine red and yellow or green peppers, asparagus, onion and coriander. Line a large serving platter with rocket or watercress, top with vegetables, squid (calamari) and scallops. Drizzle with dressing and serve immediately.*

Serves 4

home smoked trout

Method:

1 *Place smoking chips and wine in a non-reactive metal dish and stand for 1 hour.*

2 *Preheat covered barbecue to a low heat. Place dish, with smoking chips in, in barbecue over hot coals, cover barbecue with lid and heat for 5-10 minutes or until liquid is hot.*

3 *Place trout on a wire rack set in a roasting tin. Brush trout lightly with oil, then top with onions, lemon and dill. Position roasting tin containing trout on rack in barbecue, cover barbecue with lid and smoke for 15-20 minutes or until trout flakes when tested with fork.*

Note: *This recipe is also suitable for a smoke box.*

Serves 4

ingredients

1 cup/125g/4oz smoking chips
$^1/_2$ cup/125mL/4fl oz white wine
4 small rainbow trout, cleaned, with head and tail intact
1 tablespoon vegetable oil
3 red onions, thinly sliced
1 lemon, thinly sliced
8 sprigs dill

salmon
skewers

Method:

1. *Preheat barbecue to a medium heat. Thread salmon and snow peas (mangetout), alternately, onto lightly oiled skewers.*
2. *Place mustard, thyme, cumin, lemon juice and honey in a bowl and mix to combine. Brush mustard mixture over salmon and cook on lightly oiled barbecue grill for 2-3 minutes each side or until salmon is just cooked.*

Note: *Watch a lit barbecue at all times and keep children and pets away from hot barbecues and equipment.*

Serves 4

ingredients

500g/1 lb salmon fillet, cut into 2½cm/1in squares
250g/8oz snow peas (mangetout), trimmed
1 tablespoon wholegrain mustard
2 teaspoons chopped fresh lemon thyme or thyme
½ teaspoon ground cumin
2 tablespoons lemon juice
2 teaspoons honey

sesame prawn (shrimp) cakes

Photograph page 25

ingredients

315g/10oz uncooked, shelled and deveined prawns (shrimp)
250g/8oz fresh crab meat
3 spring onions, chopped
2 tablespoons finely chopped fresh basil
1 fresh red chilli, finely chopped
1 teaspoon ground cumin
1 teaspoon paprika
1 egg white
155g/5oz sesame seeds
1 tablespoon vegetable oil

Method:

1 *Preheat barbecue to a medium heat. Place prawns (shrimp), crab meat, spring onions, basil, chilli, cumin, paprika and egg white into a food processor and process until well combined. Take 4 tablespoons of mixture, shape into a pattie and roll in sesame seeds to coat. Repeat with remaining mixture to make six patties.*

2 *Heat oil on barbecue plate (griddle) for 2-3 minutes or until hot, add patties and cook for 10 minutes each side or until patties are golden and cooked.*

Note: *If fresh crab meat is unavailable drained canned crab can be used instead. These fish cakes are delicious served with a sweet chilli sauce for dipping. Sweet chilli sauce is available from Oriental food shops and some supermarkets.*

Serves 6

lemon grass prawns (shrimp)

Photograph page 25

ingredients

1 kg/2 lb uncooked medium prawns (shrimp)
3 stalks fresh lemon grass, finely chopped
2 spring onions, chopped
2 small fresh red chillies, finely chopped
2 cloves garlic, crushed
2 tablespoons finely grated fresh ginger
1 teaspoon shrimp paste
1 tablespoon brown sugar
$^1/_2$ cup/125mL/4fl oz coconut milk

Method:

1 *Wash prawns (shrimp), leaving shells and heads intact and place in a shallow glass or ceramic dish.*

2 *Place lemon grass, spring onions, chillies, garlic, ginger and shrimp paste in a food processor or blender and process until smooth. Add sugar and coconut milk and process to combine. Spoon mixture over prawns, toss to combine, cover and marinate in the refrigerator for 3-4 hours.*

3 *Preheat barbecue to a high heat. Drain prawns (shrimp), place on barbecue and cook, turning several times, for 5 minutes or until prawns (shrimp) change colour. Serve immediately.*

Note: *Fresh lemon grass and shrimp paste are available from Oriental food shops and some supermarkets. Lemon grass can also be purchased dried; if using dried lemon grass, soak it in hot water for 20 minutes or until soft before using.*

Serves 4

blackened
tuna steaks

Method:

1. *Preheat barbecue to a high heat. To make salsa, place tomatoes, fennel, onion, capers, mint, garlic, lemon juice and orange juice in a bowl and toss to combine. Set aside until ready to serve.*
2. *To make spice mix, place paprika, ground garlic, onion powder, black peppercorns, herbs and cayenne pepper in a bowl and mix to combine. Add tuna, toss to coat and shake off excess.*
3. *Heat oil on barbecue plate (griddle) for 2-3 minutes or until hot, add tuna and cook for 3-4 minutes each side or until blackened and cooked to your liking. Serve immediately with salsa.*

Note: *If tuna is unavailable swordfish or salmon are delicious alternatives. Dried ground garlic is available in the spice section of supermarkets. It has a pungent taste and smell and should be used with care.*

Serves 4

ingredients

4 thick tuna steaks
2 tablespoons olive oil

Cajun spice mix
2 tablespoons sweet paprika
1 tablespoon dried ground garlic
1 tablespoon onion powder
2 teaspoons crushed black peppercorns
2 teaspoons dried mixed herbs
1 teaspoon cayenne pepper

Fennel tomato salsa
4 plum (egg or Italian tomatoes), chopped
1 bulb fennel, finely chopped
1 red onion, finely chopped
2 tablespoons capers
1 tablespoon chopped fresh mint
1 clove garlic, crushed
1 tablespoon lemon juice
1 tablespoon orange juice

oysters and mussels in shells

Method:

1 *Preheat barbecue to a high heat. Place mussels and oysters on barbecue grill and cook for 3-5 minutes or until mussel shells open and oysters are warm. Discard any mussels that do not open after 5 minutes cooking.*
2 *Place butter, parsley, lemon juice, orange juice and wine in a heavy-based saucepan, place on barbecue and cook, stirring, for 2 minutes or until mixture is bubbling. Place mussels and oysters on a serving platter, drizzle with butter mixture and serve immediately.*

Note: *Mussels will live out of water for up to 7 days if treated correctly. To keep mussels alive, place them in a bucket, cover with a wet towel and top with ice. Store in a cool place and as the ice melts, drain off the water and replace ice. It is important that the mussels do not sit in the water or they will drown.*

Serves 6

ingredients

500g/1 lb mussels, scrubbed and beards removed
24 oysters in half shells
60g/2oz butter, softened
1 tablespoon chopped fresh parsley
2 tablespoons lemon juice
1 tablespoon orange juice
1 tablespoon white wine

cranberry chicken skewers

perfect poultry

This exciting selection of recipes

for chicken, duck and quail are sure to become barbecue favourites. Included are such tempting dishes as Cranberry Chicken Skewers, Plum Duck Salad and Festive Smoked Turkey.

cranberry chicken skewers

Photograph page 29

ingredients

750g/1$^1/_2$ lb ground chicken meat
$^1/_2$ cup/30g/1oz breadcrumbs, made from stale bread
1 onion, diced
2 cloves garlic, crushed
2 tablespoons chopped fresh sage or 1 teaspoon dried sage
1 teaspoon ground mixed spice
1 egg, lightly beaten
$^1/_4$ teaspoon Tabasco sauce or according to taste
$^1/_2$ cup/125mL/4fl oz cranberry sauce, warmed

Method:

1. *Place ground chicken meat, breadcrumbs, onion, garlic, sage, mixed spice, egg and Tabasco sauce in a bowl and mix to combine.*
2. *Shape chicken mixture around lightly oiled skewers to form 7$^1/_2$cm/3in sausage shapes. Place skewers on a plate, cover and refrigerate for 2 hours.*
3. *Preheat barbecue to a medium heat. Place skewers on lightly oiled barbecue grill and cook, turning several times, for 5-10 minutes or until skewers are cooked. Drizzle with cranberry sauce and serve immediately.*

Note: *Remember always check the barbecue area before lighting the barbecue. Do not have the barbecue too close to the house and sweep up any dry leaves or anything that might catch fire if hit by a spark.*

Serves 6

oriental chicken livers

ingredients

125g/4oz chicken livers, trimmed, cleaned and cut into sixteen pieces
8 water chestnuts, halved
8 rashers bacon, rind removed and cut in half

Oriental marinade

1 teaspoon brown sugar
1 tablespoon hot water
2 tablespoons soy sauce
1 tablespoon oyster sauce
$^1/_2$ teaspoon five spice powder
2 cloves garlic, crushed

Method:

1. *To make marinade, place sugar and water in a bowl and mix to dissolve sugar. Add soy sauce, oyster sauce, five spice powder and garlic and mix to combine. Add chicken livers, cover and marinate in the refrigerator for 3 hours.*
2. *Preheat barbecue to a high heat. Drain livers well. Place a piece of liver and water chestnut on each piece of bacon and wrap to enclose. Secure with a wooden toothpick or cocktail stick. Place on lightly oiled barbecue grill and cook, turning several times, for 6-8 minutes or until bacon is crisp and livers are just cooked.*

Note: *Heat the barbecue plate (griddle) or grill and brush lightly with oil before adding the food. This will prevent the food sticking to the barbecue. Remember when brushing with oil to use a brush that can withstand heat - if you use one with nylon bristles they will melt.*

Makes 16

chilli
honey drumsticks

Method:

1. *To make marinade, place lemon juice, honey, garlic and chilli powder in a bowl and mix to combine.*
2. *Place drumsticks in a shallow glass or ceramic dish, pour marinade over and toss to coat. Cover and marinate in the refrigerator for at least 2 hours, or overnight, turning several times during marinating.*
3. *Preheat barbecue to a medium heat. Drain drumsticks and reserve marinade. Cook drumsticks on lightly oiled barbecue, brushing frequently with marinade for 10-15 minutes, or until chicken is tender.*

Serves 10

ingredients

10 chicken drumsticks

Chilli honey marinade

1/2 cup/125 mL/4fl oz lemon juice
1/2 cup/170g/5 1/2oz honey
1 clove garlic, crushed
pinch chilli powder

caribbean
spatchcock

Method:

1 *To make marinade, place rum, lime rind, lime juice, honey, garlic and ginger in a bowl and mix to combine. Place spatchcock (poussin) halves in a shallow glass or ceramic dish and rub marinade into spatchcocks (poussins). Cover and set aside to marinate for 1 hour.*

2 *Preheat barbecue to a medium heat. Thread a skewer through wings and legs of each spatchcock (poussin) half and brush with any remaining marinade. Combine black pepper and coriander and press onto skin of birds. Cook on lightly oiled barbecue grill, turning frequently for 15-20 minutes or until birds are cooked through.*

Cook's tip: *This is also a delicious way to prepare and cook chicken pieces. Instead of using spatchcocks, simply use chicken pieces and prepare and marinate as in this recipe - the cooking time for the chicken pieces will be about the same as for the spatchcocks. You should cook them until the juices run clear.*

Serves 6

ingredients

3 spatchcocks (poussins), halved
2 tablespoons cracked black pepper
1 teaspoon ground coriander

Lime marinade
3 tablespoons white rum
2 teaspoons finely grated lime rind
1 tablespoon lime juice
2 tablespoons honey
2 cloves garlic, crushed
1 teaspoon grated fresh ginger

cajun
chicken with lime sauce

Method:

1 *Preheat barbecue to a high heat.*
2 *To make spice mix, place garlic, paprika, oregano, thyme, salt and black pepper in a bowl and mix to combine. Add chicken and toss to coat. Shake off excess spice mix and cook, turning frequently, on lightly oiled barbecue plate (griddle) for 5-7 minutes or until chicken is tender.*
3 *To make sauce, place yoghurt, lime juice, lime rind and cordial in a bowl and mix to combine. Serve with chicken.*

Note: *For an attractive presentation, place a bowl of dipping sauce in the centre of a serving platter, surround with chicken and garnish with lime wedges.*

Serves 6

ingredients

4 boneless chicken breast fillets, cut into 2cm/$^3/_4$in wide strips

Cajun spice mix
5 cloves garlic, crushed
4 tablespoons paprika
2 tablespoons dried oregano
2 tablespoons dried thyme
2 teaspoons salt
2 teaspoons freshly ground black pepper

Lime dipping
1$^1/_2$ cups/315g/10oz low-fat natural yoghurt
2 tablespoons fresh lime juice
1 tablespoon finely grated lime rind
1 teaspoon lime juice cordial

chilli
lime legs

Photograph page 35

Method:

chicken
with creamy pesto stuffing

Method:

1 *To make stuffing, place basil leaves, pine nuts and Parmesan cheese in a food processor and process to finely chopped. Stir basil mixture into cream cheese.*

2 *Cut through backbone of each chicken. Remove both halves of backbone, then turn chicken over and press to flatten.*

3 *Using your fingers or the handle of a wooden spoon, loosen skin over breasts, thighs and legs of chicken. Push stuffing under loosened skin, then thread skewers through wings and legs of chickens.*

4 *Preheat barbecue to a medium heat. Cook chicken on lightly oiled barbecue for 15-20 minutes each side or until chicken is cooked through.*

When is the chicken cooked?

To test your chicken for doneness pierce the thickest part of the chicken at the thigh joint and when the juices run clear the bird is cooked.

Serves 10

ingredients

3 x 1½ kg/3 lb chickens

Creaming pesto stuffing

90g/3oz basil leaves

60g/2oz pine nuts

½ cup/60g/2oz finely grated Parmesan cheese

250g/8oz cream cheese, softened

undercover chicken

Method:

1. *Preheat covered barbecue to a medium heat. Wash chicken inside and out and pat dry with absorbent kitchen paper.*
2. *Place butter, garlic, chives and parsley in a bowl and mix to combine. Using your fingers, loosen skin on breast of chicken. Push butter mixture under skin and smooth out evenly. Place chicken on a wire rack set in a roasting tin and brush with oil. Place prosciutto or ham over chicken breast in a criss-cross pattern and secure in place with wooden toothpicks or cocktail sticks. Pour wine over chicken.*
3. *Place roasting tin on rack in barbecue, cover barbecue with lid and cook for 1½ hours or until chicken is tender. Cover and stand for 10 minutes before carving.*

   Note: *Do not handle cooked and uncooked meat and poultry at the same time. This encourages the transfer of bacteria from raw food to cooked food. Always make sure that you have a clean tray or dish to place barbecued food on - do not place it on the same dish as was used for holding it raw - unless it has been thoroughly washed in hot soapy water.*

Serves 6

ingredients

1½ kg/3 lb chicken, cleaned
125 g/4 oz butter, softened
1 clove garlic, crushed
2 tablespoons snipped fresh chives
2 tablespoons chopped fresh parsley
1 tablespoon olive oil
8 slices prosciutto or lean ham
1 cup/250mL/8fl oz white wine

tikka skewers

ingredients

750g/1½ lb firm white fish fillets, cut into 2cm/¾in wide strips
1 lemon, cut into wedges

Spicy yoghurt marinade
1 onion, chopped
4 cloves garlic, crushed
2 teaspoons finely grated fresh ginger
1 tablespoon ground cumin
1 tablespoon garam masala
3 cardamom pods, crushed
1 teaspoon ground turmeric
2 teaspoons chilli powder
2 teaspoons ground coriander
1 tablespoon tomato paste (purée)
1¾ cups/350g/11oz natural yogurt

Cucumber raitha
1 cucumber, finely chopped
1 tablespoon chopped fresh mint
1 cup/200g/6½oz natural yogurt

Method:

1. *Pierce fish strips several times with a fork and place in a shallow glass or ceramic dish.*
2. *To make marinade, place onion, garlic, ginger, cumin, garam masala, cardamom, turmeric, chilli powder, coriander and tomato paste (purée) in a food processor or blender and process until smooth. Add yoghurt and mix to combine. Spoon marinade over fish, toss to combine, cover and marinate in the refrigerator for 3 hours.*
3. *Preheat barbecue to a medium heat. Drain fish and thread onto lightly oiled skewers. Place skewers on lightly oiled barbecue grill and cook, turning several times, for 5-6 minutes or until fish is cooked.*
4. *To make raitha, place cucumber, mint and yoghurt in a bowl and mix to combine. Serve skewers with lemon wedges and raitha.*

Note: *When buying fish fillets look for those that are shiny and firm with a pleasant sea smell. Avoid those that are dull, soft, discoloured or oozing water when touched.*

Serves 6

fragrant orange quail

Method:

1. *To make marinade, place herbs, mustard, orange rind, garlic, cider, orange juice, brandy and oil in a shallow glass or ceramic dish and mix to combine. Add quail, turn to coat, cover and marinate in the refrigerator for 2 hours.*
2. *Preheat barbecue to a medium heat. Drain quail, place skin side up, on lightly oiled barbecue grill and cook, turning occasionally, for 10 minutes or until quail is tender.*
3. *For couscous, place couscous in a bowl, pour over boiling water, cover and set aside to stand for 10 minutes or until water is absorbed. Toss with a fork, add sultanas, hazelnuts, spring onions and lemon juice and toss to combine. To serve, line a large serving platter with couscous then arrange quail attractively on top.*

   Note: *Often thought of as a type of grain couscous is actually a pasta made from durum wheat, however cook and use it in the same way as a grain. The name couscous refers to both the raw product and the cooked dish. It is an excellent source of thiamin and iron as well as being a good source of protein and niacin.*

   Serves 4

ingredients

6 quail, halved

Brandy orange marinade
6 tablespoons chopped fresh mixed herbs
2 tablespoons Dijon mustard
1 tablespoon finely grated orange rind
2 cloves garlic, crushed
1/2 cup/125mL/4fl oz cider
1/2 cup/125mL/4fl oz orange juice
1/4 cup/60mL/2fl oz brandy
1 tablespoon macadamia or walnut oil

Nutty couscous
1 cup/185g/6oz couscous
2 cups/500mL/16fl oz boiling water
90g/3oz sultanas
60g/2oz hazelnuts, toasted and chopped
2 spring onions, chopped
1 tablespoon lemon juice

chicken in coals

Photograph page 41

ingredients

1½ kg/3 lb chicken
60g/2oz butter, melted
2 tablespoons soy sauce
1 tablespoon honey
2 star anise
1 cinnamon stick

Method:

1. *Heat barbecue until flames die down and coals are glowing. The barbecue is ready when you can hold your hand about 10cm/4in from the coals for 4-5 seconds.*
2. *Cut chicken down back bone and press to flatten. Place butter, soy sauce and honey in a bowl and mix to combine. Brush butter mixture over chicken and place on a sheet of nonstick baking paper large enough to completely enclose chicken. Top chicken with star anise and cinnamon stick and wrap in baking paper. Then wrap paper parcel in a double thickness of aluminium foil.*
3. *Place chicken in coals and cook, turning several times, for 45-60 minutes or until chicken is cooked and tender.*

***Note:** For this recipe the chicken is actually cooked in the coals of the barbecue so it is important that the fire is not too hot. If using wood the fire should burn down to red hot glowing embers. When using charcoal or heat beads the coals should be glowing and partially covered by grey ash. Charcoal takes 15-20 minutes to reach this stage, heat beads 30-40 minutes and wood an hour or more, depending on the variety used.*

Serves 4

---

indian yoghurt kebabs

Photograph page 41

ingredients

6 chicken thigh fillets, halved

Yoghurt marinade
1 tablespoon chopped fresh coriander
2 teaspoons finely grated fresh ginger
1 clove garlic, crushed
2 teaspoons paprika
1 teaspoon ground cumin
½ teaspoon ground turmeric
½ teaspoon chilli powder
½ teaspoon ground cinnamon
1 cup/200g/6½oz natural yoghurt
2 tablespoons lemon juice

Method:

1. *To make marinade, place coriander, ginger, garlic, paprika, cumin, turmeric, chilli powder, cinnamon, yoghurt and lemon juice in a shallow glass or ceramic dish and mix well to combine. Add chicken, toss to coat and marinate at room temperature for 30 minutes.*
2. *Preheat barbecue to a medium heat. Drain chicken and thread three pieces onto a lightly oiled skewer. Repeat with remaining chicken to make four kebabs. Place kebabs on lightly oiled barbecue grill and cook for 4-5 minutes each side or until chicken is cooked and tender.*

***Note:** If chicken thigh fillets are unavailable chicken breast fillets can be used instead. You will need 3 boneless chicken breast fillets, each cut into four pieces.*

Serves 4

41

43

festive
smoked turkey

Method:

1. *Soak smoking chips in brandy in a non-reactive metal dish for 1 hour.*

ingredients

1 cup/125g/4oz smoking chips

make
mine
meat

thai lamb noodle salad

make mine meat

Here you will find new ways to

make the most of your favourite cuts of meat. Why not try a Marinated Leg of Lamb or Mixed Satays at your next barbecue.

thai lamb
and noodle salad

Photograph page 45

ingredients

1 stalk fresh lemon grass, chopped or $^1/_2$ teaspoon dried lemon grass, soaked in hot water until soft
2 cloves garlic, crushed
$^1/_4$ cup/60mL/2fl oz lime juice
2 tablespoons vegetable oil
2 tablespoons sweet chilli sauce
1 tablespoon fish sauce
750g/1$^1/_2$ lb lamb fillets, trimmed of excess fat and sinew

Rice noodle salad
155g/5oz rice noodles
6 spring onions, chopped
1 red pepper, chopped
60g/2oz bean sprouts
3 tablespoons fresh coriander leaves

Lime and chilli dressing
$^1/_4$ cup/60mL/2fl oz lime juice
1 tablespoon fish sauce
1 tablespoon honey
pinch chilli powder or according to taste

Method:

1. *Combine lemon grass, garlic, lime juice, oil, chilli sauce and fish sauce in a glass or ceramic dish and mix to combine. Add lamb, turn to coat, cover and marinate in the refrigerator for 3 hours.*
2. *Preheat barbecue to a medium heat. To make salad, prepare noodles according to packet directions. Drain and place in a bowl. Add spring onions, red pepper, bean sprouts and coriander and toss to combine. Set aside.*
3. *To make dressing, place lime juice, fish sauce, honey and chilli powder in a screwtop jar and shake well to combine. Set aside.*
4. *Drain lamb and cook on lightly oiled barbecue, turning several times, for 5-10 minutes or until cooked to your liking. Slice lamb diagonally into 2cm/$^3/_4$in thick slices.*
5. *To serve, place salad on a large serving platter, arrange lamb attractively on top and drizzle with dressing. Serve immediately.*

Note: *Rice noodles, also called rice vermicelli or rice sticks, vary in size from a narrow vermicelli style to a ribbon noodle about 5 mm/1/4 in wide. Made from rice flour, the noodles should be soaked before using; the narrow noodles require about 10 minutes soaking, while the wider ones will need about 30 minutes.*

Serves 6

lamb
with honeyed onions

Method:

1. *To make marinade, place mint, garlic, yoghurt, mustard and mint sauce in a shallow glass or ceramic dish and mix to combine. Add lamb, turn to coat, cover and marinate in the refrigerator for 3 hours.*
2. *Preheat barbecue to a medium heat. For Honeyed Onions, heat oil on barbecue plate (griddle), add onions and cook, stirring constantly, for 10 minutes. Add honey and vinegar and cook, stirring, for 5 minutes longer or until onions are very soft and golden.*
3. *Drain lamb, place on lightly oiled barbecue and cook for 2-3 minutes each side or until cooked to your liking. Serve with onions.*

   Note: *Before lighting a gas barbecue check that all the gas fittings and hose connections are tight and fitting correctly.*

   Serves 6

ingredients

12 lamb cutlets, trimmed of excess fat

Yoghurt marinade
1 tablespoon chopped fresh mint
1 clove garlic, crushed
1 cup/200 g/61/2 oz low-fat natural yoghurt
2 tablespoons wholegrain mustard
1 tablespoon prepared mint sauce

Honeyed onions
2 tablespoons olive oil
2 red onions, sliced
1 tablespoon honey
2 tablespoons red wine vinegar

mixed
satays

ingredients

250g/8oz chicken breast fillets, skin removed and sliced into thin strips, lengthwise
250g/8oz beef fillet, sliced into thin strips, lengthwise
250g/8oz pork fillet, sliced into thin strips, lengthwise
12 skewers, lightly oiled

Chilli marinade
1/4 cup/60mL/2fl oz soy sauce
2 tablespoons lime or lemon juice
2 cloves garlic, crushed
2 teaspoons finely grated fresh ginger
1 fresh red chilli, finely chopped
1 tablespoon finely chopped fresh coriander

Peanut sauce
1/2 cup/125g/4oz crunchy peanut butter
1 onion, finely chopped
2 tablespoons hoisin sauce
2 cloves garlic, crushed
1/2 cup/125mL/4fl oz coconut milk
2 tablespoons finely chopped fresh coriander

Method:

1. *Weave chicken, beef and pork strips onto skewers and place in a shallow glass or ceramic dish.*
2. *To make marinade, place soy sauce, lime or lemon juice, garlic, ginger, chilli and coriander in a small bowl and mix to combine. Pour marinade over skewers in dish, cover and set aside to marinate for at least 1 hour.*
3. *Preheat barbecue to a medium heat. Cook kebabs on lightly oiled barbecue, turning frequently for 5-6 minutes, or until meats are cooked.*
4. *To make sauce, place peanut butter, onion, hoisin sauce, garlic and coconut milk in a food processor or blender and process until smooth. Stir in coriander. Serve with skewers for dipping.*

Makes 12 skewers

barbecued steak sandwiches

Method:

1. *To make marinade, place wine, oil, garlic and ginger in a bowl and mix to combine. Place steaks in a shallow glass or ceramic dish. Pour marinade over, cover, and marinate at room temperature for 2-3 hours or overnight in the refrigerator.*
2. *Cook onions on lightly oiled barbecue plate (griddle) or in a lightly oiled frying pan on barbecue for 10-15 minutes or until golden.Preheat barbecue to a medium heat. Drain steaks and cook on lightly oiled barbecue for 3-5 minutes each side or until cooked to your liking.*
3. *Lightly brush bread slices with oil and cook on barbecue grill for 1-2 minutes each side or until lightly toasted. To assemble sandwiches, top 6 toasted bread slices with steak, onions and remaining bread slices.*

Cook's tip: *You may like to add some salad ingredients to your sandwiches. Mustard or relish is also a tasty addition.*

Marinated steak, barbecued and placed between slices of grilled bread makes the best steak sandwiches you will ever taste.

Serves 6

ingredients

6 lean rump steaks, cut 1cm/½in thick
3 onions, finely sliced
12 thick slices wholemeal or grain bread
olive oil

Ginger wine marinade

1 cup/250mL/8fl oz red wine
½ cup/125mL/4fl oz olive oil
1 clove garlic, crushed
2 teaspoons grated fresh ginger

lamb
cutlets with honey butter

Method:

1 *To make Honey Butter, place butter, mint, honey and black pepper to taste in a small bowl and mix to combine. Place mixture on plastic food wrap and roll into a cylindrical shape. Refrigerate until hard.*

2 *Preheat barbecue to a medium heat. Place oil and garlic in a small bowl and mix to combine. Wrap ends of cutlet bones in aluminium foil to prevent burning during cooking. Brush cutlets with oil mixture and cook on barbecue plate (griddle) for 3 minutes each side or until lamb is tender.*

3 *Cut butter into small rounds and serve with cutlets.*

Cook's tip: *Interesting butter shapes can be made by using small cookie cutter shapes.*

Serves 4

ingredients

1 tablespoon vegetable oil
1 clove garlic, crushed
8 lamb cutlets

Honey butter
90g/3oz butter, softened
2 tablespoons chopped fresh mint
1 tablespoon honey
freshly ground black pepper

pork steaks
with apple stuffing

Method:

1. *Place butterfly steaks on a board and, using a meat mallet, flatten slightly.*
2. *To make stuffing, melt butter in a frying pan and cook onion and bacon for 4-5 minutes or until bacon is crisp. Add apple and cook until apple is soft. Place apple mixture in a bowl, add bread crumbs, egg, mozzarella cheese and parsley and mix to combine. Season to taste with black pepper.*
3. *Preheat barbecue to a medium heat. Place spoonfuls of stuffing on one side of each butterfly steak, then fold over and secure with toothpicks. Cook on lightly oiled barbecue for 5-6 minutes each side or until steaks are cooked.*

Serves 6

ingredients

6 pork butterfly steaks

Apple stuffing
30g/1oz butter
1 onion, finely chopped
2 rashers bacon, finely chopped
1 apple, cored and finely chopped
1½ cups/90g/3oz bread crumbs, made from stale bread
1 egg, lightly beaten
155g/5oz mozzarella cheese, cut into small cubes
2 tablespoons chopped fresh parsley
freshly ground black pepper

fruity barbecued lamb

Photograph page 53

ingredients

4 lamb shanks (knuckles)
2 tablespoons mango chutney
2 cloves garlic, crushed
1 tablespoon finely grated fresh ginger
1/4 cup/60mL/2fl oz apple juice
1/4 cup/60ml/2fl oz white wine
2 tablespoons olive oil
4 bulbs young garlic, cut in half horizontally

Method:

1. *Score the thickest part of each lamb shank (knuckle) to allow for even cooking.*
2. *Place chutney, crushed garlic, ginger, apple juice, wine and oil in a shallow ovenproof glass, ceramic or enamel dish and mix to combine. Add lamb, turn to coat, cover and marinate in the refrigerator for 2 hours. Remove lamb from refrigerator and bake in oven for 1 hour.*
3. *Preheat barbecue to a medium heat. Remove lamb from baking dish and place on lightly oiled barbecue, add garlic bulbs and cook, turning occasionally, for 30 minutes or until lamb and garlic are tender.*

Note: *Use fresh young garlic for this recipe, its flavour is milder than more mature garlic and when cooked develops a delicious nutty taste. Lamb chops are also delicious cooked in this way, however no precooking is required and the cooking time on the barbecue will only be 3-5 minutes each side.*

Serves 4

Oven temperature 180°C, 350°F, Gas 4

---

rosemary and thyme chops

Photograph page 53

ingredients

12 lamb neck chops, trimmed of excess fat

Fresh herb marinade
2 tablespoons chopped fresh rosemary
2 tablespoons chopped fresh thyme
2 cloves garlic, crushed
1/4 cup/60mL/2fl oz olive oil
1/4 cup/60mL/2fl oz balsamic or red wine vinegar
2 tablespoons lime juice

Method:

1. *To make marinade, place rosemary, thyme, garlic, oil, vinegar and lime juice in a shallow glass or ceramic dish and mix to combine. Add lamb, turn to coat, cover and marinate at room temperature for 1 hour.*
2. *Preheat barbecue to a high heat. Drain lamb, place on lightly oiled barbecue and cook for 3-5 minutes each side or until chops are cooked to your liking.*

Note: *Long-handled tongs are a must for turning food without burning your hands.*

Serves 6

steaks
with blue butter

ingredients

1 tablespoon freshly ground black pepper
2 tablespoons olive oil
6 fillet steaks, trimmed of excess fat

Blue butter
125g/4oz butter, softened
60g/2oz blue cheese
1 tablespoon chopped fresh parsley
1 teaspoon paprika

Method:

1. *To make Blue Butter, place butter, blue cheese, parsley and paprika in a bowl and beat to combine. Place butter on a piece of plastic food wrap and roll into a log shape. Refrigerate for 1 hour or until firm.*
2. *Preheat barbecue to a high heat.*
3. *Place black pepper and oil in a bowl and mix to combine. Brush steaks lightly with oil mixture. Place steaks on lightly oiled barbecue grill and cook for 3-5 minutes each side or until steaks are cooked to your liking.*
4. *Cut butter into 2cm/¾in thick slices and top each steak with 1 or 2 slices. Serve immediately.*

Note: *Any leftover Blue Butter can be stored in the freezer to use at a later date. It is also delicious served with grilled lamb chops or cutlets and grilled vegetables such as eggplant (aubergine), red and green peppers and zucchini (courgettes).*

Serves 6

beef
and bacon burgers

Method:

1 *Preheat barbecue to a medium heat. Place beef, spring onions, chives, egg, tomato sauce, Worcestershire sauce and chilli sauce in a bowl and mix to combine. Shape mixture into twelve patties. Top six patties with mozzarella cheese, then with remaining patties and pinch edges together to seal. Wrap a piece of bacon around each pattie and secure with a wooden toothpick or cocktail stick. Place on a plate and refrigerate for 2 hours or until patties are firm.*

2 *Place patties in a lightly oiled hinged wire barbecue frame and cook on barbecue grill for 10-15 minutes or until patties are cooked to your liking and cheese melts.*

Note: *A hinged wire frame is a useful barbecue accessory. It is ideal for cooking fragile and delicate foods such as fish - whole, fillets and cutlets - and burgers which can fall apart when turning.*

Serves 6

ingredients

750g/1 1/2 lb lean ground beef
3 spring onions, chopped
2 tablespoons snipped fresh chives
1 egg, lightly beaten
2 tablespoons tomato sauce
1 tablespoon Worcestershire sauce
1 tablespoon chilli sauce
125g/4oz grated mozzarella cheese
6 rashers bacon, rind removed

cajun
spiced steaks

Method:

1 *Preheat barbecue to a high heat. To make salsa, place pineapple, spring onions, coriander, chilli, sugar and vinegar in a bowl and toss to combine. Set aside.*

2 *To make spice mixture, combine paprika, black peppercorns, thyme, oregano and chilli powder. Rub spice mixture over steaks. Place steaks on lightly oiled barbecue and cook for 3-5 minutes each side or until cooked to your liking. Serve with salsa.*

Note: *When testing to see if a steak is cooked to your liking, press it with a pair of blunt tongs. Do not cut the meat, as this causes the juices to escape. Rare steaks will feel springy, medium steaks slightly springy and well-done steaks will feel firm. As a guide a 2.5 cm/1 in thick steak cooked to rare takes about 3 minutes each side, a medium steak 4 minutes and a well-done steak 5 minutes.*

Serves 4

ingredients

4 sirloin or fillet steaks, trimmed of excess fat

Cajun spice mixture
1 tablespoon sweet paprika
1 teaspoon crushed black peppercorns
1 teaspoon ground thyme
1 teaspoon ground oregano
1/4 teaspoon chilli powder

Pineapple chilli salsa
1/2 pineapple, peeled and chopped
2 spring onions, chopped
1 tablespoon chopped fresh coriander
1 fresh red chilli, chopped
1 tablespoon brown sugar
1 tablespoon white vinegar

korean
bulgogi

Method:

1. *Place garlic, ginger, soy sauce, honey and chilli sauce in a bowl and mix to combine. Add beef, toss to coat, cover and marinate in the refrigerator for 4 hours.*
2. *Preheat barbecue to a high heat. Heat 1 tablespoon oil on barbecue plate (griddle), add beef and stir-fry for 1-2 minutes or until beef just changes colour. Push beef to side of barbecue to keep warm.*
3. *Heat remaining oil on barbecue plate (griddle), add onions and bean sprouts and stir-fry for 4-5 minutes or until onions are golden. Add beef to onion mixture and stir-fry for 1-2 minutes longer. Sprinkle with sesame seeds and serve immediately.*

Note: *Serve with steamed white or brown rice and a tossed green salad.*

Serves 6

ingredients

4 cloves garlic, crushed
2 teaspoons finely grated fresh ginger
1/4 cup/60mL/2fl oz soy sauce
3 tablespoons honey
1 tablespoon sweet chilli sauce
750g/1 1/2 lb rump steak, trimmed of visible fat and thinly sliced
2 tablespoons vegetable oil
2 onions, sliced
125g/4oz bean sprouts
2 tablespoons sesame seeds

vegetarian variety

barbecued pumpkin pizza

vegetarian variety

Given the number of people who now

choose to be vegetarians or semi-vegetarians it is a good idea to serve a vegetarian alternative - these recipes fit the bill and are sure to be popular with everyone.

char-grilled mushrooms and toast

Method:

1 *Preheat barbecue to a medium heat. Brush mushrooms with oil and cook on lightly oiled barbecue for 4-5 minutes or until cooked. Brush both sides of the bread with remaining oil and cook for 2-3 minutes each side or until golden.*

2 *Rub one side of each bread slice with cut side of garlic clove. Top each slice of bread with mushrooms, sprinkle with parsley, chives and basil. Season to taste with black pepper and serve immediately.*

Note: *This delicious first course takes only minutes to cook.*

Serves 2

ingredients

6 flat mushrooms
$^1/_4$ cup/60mL/2fl oz olive oil
2 thick slices of bread
1 clove garlic, cut in half
2 teaspoons finely chopped fresh parsley
2 teaspoons snipped fresh chives
1 teaspoon finely chopped fresh basil
freshly ground black pepper

vegetable
burgers

ingredients

10 wholemeal rolls, split
10 lettuce leaves

Mixed vegetable patties
500g/1 lb broccoli, chopped
500g/1 lb zucchini (courgettes), chopped
250g/8oz carrots, chopped
2 onions, finely chopped
2 cloves garlic, crushed
3 tablespoons chopped parsley
3 cups/185g/6oz dried bread crumbs
1/2 cup/60g/2oz flour, sifted
freshly ground black pepper

Spicy tomato sauce
1 tablespoon olive oil
1 onion, finely chopped
1 clove garlic, crushed
1 fresh red chilli, seeded and finely chopped
1 green pepper, finely chopped
440g/14oz canned tomatoes, undrained and mashed
freshly ground black pepper

Method:

1 *To make patties, boil, steam or microwave broccoli, zucchini (courgettes) and carrots until tender. Drain, rinse under cold running water and pat dry.*

2 *Place broccoli, zucchini (courgettes), carrots, onions, garlic and parsley in a food processor and process until puréed. Transfer vegetable mixture to a mixing bowl, add bread crumbs and flour, season with black pepper and mix to combine. Cover and refrigerate for 30 minutes.*

3 *Shape mixture into ten patties. Place on a tray lined with nonstick baking paper, cover and refrigerate until required.*

4 *To make sauce, heat oil in a saucepan and cook onion, garlic, chilli and green pepper for 5 minutes or until onion and green pepper are soft. Add tomatoes, bring mixture to the boil, then reduce heat and simmer for 15-20 minutes or until sauce thickens. Season to taste with black pepper.*

5 *Preheat barbecue to a medium heat. Cook patties on lightly oiled barbecue plate (griddle) or in a lightly oiled frying pan on barbecue for 3-4 minutes each side. Toast rolls on barbecue. Place a lettuce leaf, a pattie, and a spoonful of sauce on the bottom half of each roll, top with remaining roll half and serve immediately.*

Makes 10 burgers

char-grilled vegetable slices

Method:

1. *Preheat barbecue to a medium heat. Place oil and garlic in a small bowl and whisk to combine. Brush eggplant (aubergine) slices, zucchini (courgette) slices, red pepper slices and tomato slices with oil mixture.*
2. *Cook eggplant (aubergine), zucchini (courgette) and red pepper slices on lightly oiled barbecue, turning frequently, for 4-5 minutes or until almost cooked. Add tomato slices to barbecue and cook all vegetables for 2-3 minutes longer.*

Serves 6

ingredients

$^1/_2$ cup/125mL/4fl oz olive oil
1 clove garlic, crushed
1 large eggplant (aubergine), cut lengthwise into thick slices
3 large zucchini (courgettes), cut lengthwise into thick slices
2 red peppers, cut into quarters, seeds removed
3 large firm tomatoes, cut into thick slices
freshly ground black pepper

mushroom risotto cakes

Method:

1 *Melt butter and oil together in saucepan over a medium heat, add garlic and bacon and cook, stirring, for 3 minutes or until bacon is crisp. Add leek and cook for 3 minutes or until leek is golden. Add rice and mushrooms to pan and cook, stirring, for 3 minutes longer.*

2 *Stir in 3/4 cup/185mL/6fl oz hot stock and 1/4 cup/60mL/2fl oz wine and cook, stirring constantly, over a medium heat until liquid is absorbed. Continue adding stock and wine in this way, stirring constantly and allowing liquid to be absorbed before adding more.*

3 *Remove pan from heat, add Parmesan cheese and black pepper to taste and mix to combine. Set aside to cool, then refrigerate for at least 3 hours.*

4 *Preheat barbecue to a medium heat. Shape tablespoons of rice mixture into patties. Toss in flour to coat and shake off excess. Dip patties in eggs and roll in breadcrumbs to coat. Cook patties on lightly oiled barbecue plate (griddle) for 5 minutes each side or until golden and heated through.*

Note: *These bite-sized morsels are sure to be a hit with drinks before any barbecue. They can also be cooked in a frying pan over a medium heat on the cooker top.*

For a vegetarian version of this recipe omit the bacon and use vegetable stock.

Serves 6

ingredients

30g/1oz butter
1 tablespoon olive oil
2 cloves garlic, crushed
3 rashers bacon, chopped
1 leek, thinly sliced
1 1/4 cups/280g/9oz Arborio or risotto rice
125g/4oz button mushrooms, sliced
3 cups/750mL/1 1/4pt hot chicken or vegetable stock
1 cup/250mL/8fl oz dry white wine
60g/2oz grated Parmesan cheese
freshly ground black pepper
1/4 cup/30g/1oz flour
2 eggs, lightly beaten
1 1/2 cups/90g/3oz wholemeal breadcrumbs, made from stale bread

wild
rice and bean patties

Method:

1 *Preheat barbecue to a medium heat. Place soya beans, fresh coriander, spring onions, ginger, cumin, ground coriander and turmeric into a food processor and process for 30 seconds or until mixture resembles coarse breadcrumbs. Transfer mixture to a bowl, add rice, flour and egg and mix to combine. Shape mixture into patties.*
2 *Heat oil on barbecue plate (griddle) for 2-3 minutes or until hot, add patties and cook for 5 minutes each side or until golden and heated through.*
3 *To make chilli yoghurt, place yogurt, chilli sauce and lime juice in a bowl and mix to combine. Serve with patties.*

Serves 6

ingredients

440g/14oz canned soya beans, drained and rinsed
6 tablespoons chopped fresh coriander
3 spring onions, chopped
1 tablespoon finely grated fresh ginger
1 tablespoon ground cumin
1 tablespoon ground coriander
1/2 teaspoon ground turmeric
1/2 cup/100g/3 1/2oz wild rice blend, cooked
1/2 cup/75g/2 1/2oz wholemeal flour
1 egg, lightly beaten
2 tablespoons vegetable oil

Sweet chilli yoghurt
1 cup/200g/6 1/2oz low-fat natural yoghurt
2 tablespoons sweet chilli sauce
1 tablespoon lime juice

nutty
crusted ricotta salad

Method:

1 *Place ricotta cheese in a colander lined with muslin and drain for 1 hour.*

2 *Preheat barbecue to a medium heat. Place Parmesan cheese, pine nuts, paprika, oregano and 2 tablespoons oil in a bowl and mix to combine. Press nut mixture over surface of ricotta cheese to coat.*

3 *Heat remaining oil on barbecue plate (griddle) until hot, then cook ricotta cheese, turning occasionally, for 10 minutes or until golden. Stand for 10 minutes, then cut into slices.*

4 *Line a large serving platter with salad leaves, then arrange snow pea (mangetout) sprouts or watercress, teardrop or cherry tomatoes, avocado, sun-dried tomatoes and ricotta cheese slices attractively on top.*

5 *To make dressing, place garlic, cumin, coriander, chilli flakes, oil, vinegar and honey in a bowl and whisk to combine. Drizzle over salad and serve.*

Note: *If a gas barbecue does not light first time, turn if off, wait 20 seconds and try again. This will ensure that there is no gas build-up.*

Serves 4

ingredients

315g/10oz ricotta cheese in one piece
90g/3oz grated Parmesan cheese
60g/2oz pine nuts, toasted and finely chopped
1 tablespoon sweet paprika
1 tablespoon dried oregano
4 tablespoons olive oil
315g/10oz assorted salad leaves
90g/3oz snow pea (mangetout) sprouts or watercress
185g/6oz yellow teardrop or cherry tomatoes
1 avocado, stoned, peeled and chopped
30g/1oz sun-dried tomatoes, sliced

Spiced honey dressing
2 cloves garlic, crushed
1 teaspoon ground cumin
1 teaspoon ground coriander
pinch red chilli flakes
1/4 cup/60mL/2fl oz olive oil
1 tablespoon cider vinegar
1 teaspoon honey

couscous filled mushrooms

Method:

1 *Preheat barbecue to a high heat. Place couscous in a bowl, pour over boiling water, cover and set aside to stand for 5 minutes or until water is absorbed. Add butter and toss gently with a fork.*

2 *Heat oil in a frying pan over a medium heat, add onion and garlic and cook, stirring, for 3 minutes or until onion is soft. Add garam masala and cayenne pepper and cook for 1 minute longer. Add onion mixture to couscous and toss to combine.*

3 *Fill mushrooms with couscous mixture, top with feta cheese and cook on lightly oiled barbecue grill for 5 minutes or until mushrooms are tender and cheese melts.*

Note: *If your barbecue only has a grill, use a large long-handled frying pan when a recipe calls for food to be cooked on the barbecue plate (griddle).*

Serves 4

ingredients

$^2/_3$ cup/125g/4oz couscous
$^2/_3$ cup/170mL/5$^1/_2$fl oz boiling water
15g/$^1/_2$oz butter
2 teaspoons olive oil
1 onion, chopped
2 cloves garlic, crushed
1 teaspoon garam masala
pinch cayenne pepper
12 large mushrooms, stalks removed
200g/6$^1/_2$oz feta cheese, crumbled

warm vegetable salad

Photograph page 71

ingredients

6 zucchini (courgettes), cut lengthwise into quarters
2 red onions, sliced
155g/5oz snow pea (mangetout) sprouts or watercress
1 yellow or red pepper, chopped
1 avocado, stoned, peeled and chopped

Orange dressing
2 tablespoons snipped fresh chives
1/4 cup/60mL/2fl oz orange juice
1 tablespoon white wine vinegar
2 teaspoons French mustard

Method:

1. *Preheat barbecue to a medium heat. Place zucchini (courgettes) and onions on lightly oiled barbecue and cook for 2-3 minutes each side or until golden and tender.*
2. *Arrange snow pea (mangetout) sprouts or watercress, yellow or red pepper and avocado attractively on a serving platter. Top with zucchini (courgettes) and onions.*
3. *To make dressing, place chives, orange juice, vinegar and mustard in a screwtop jar and shake well to combine. Drizzle over salad and serve immediately.*

Note: *This salad is delicious served with toasted olive bread.*

Serves 4

kebabs with herb sauce

Photograph page 71

ingredients

1 green pepper, seeded and cut into 2cm/3/4in squares
2 zucchini (courgettes), cut into 2cm/3/4in pieces
1 red onion, cut into 2cm/3/4in cubes
1 eggplant (aubergine), cut into 2cm/3/4in cubes
16 cherry tomatoes
2 tablespoons olive oil
2 tablespoons lemon juice
1 tablespoon chopped fresh oregano or 1 teaspoon dried oregano

Herb sauce
1 tablespoon chopped fresh dill
2 tablespoons snipped fresh chives
1 cup/250g/8oz sour cream
2 tablespoons lemon juice

Method:

1. *Preheat barbecue to a medium heat. Thread a piece of green pepper, zucchini (courgette), onion, eggplant (aubergine) and a tomato onto a lightly oiled skewer. Repeat with remaining vegetables to use all ingredients.*
2. *Combine oil, lemon juice and oregano and brush over kebabs. Place kebabs on lightly oiled barbecue grill and cook, turning several times, for 5-10 minutes or until vegetables are tender.*
3. *To make sauce, place dill, chives, sour cream and lemon juice in a bowl and mix to combine. Serve with kebabs.*

Note: *Always keep water close at hand when barbecuing. If a hose or tap is not close by, then have a bucket of water next to the barbecue. A fire extinguisher or fire blanket is also a sensible safety precaution.*

Serves 4

grilled
pepper polenta

Method:

1 *Place water in a saucepan and bring to the boil. Reduce heat to simmering, then gradually whisk in corn meal (polenta) and cook, stirring, for 20 minutes or until mixture is thick and leaves the sides of the pan.*
2 *Stir in butter, black peppercorns and grated Parmesan cheese. Spread mixture evenly into a greased 18x28cm/7x11in shallow cake tin and refrigerate until set. Cut polenta in triangles.*
3 *Brush polenta and vegetables with oil, then cook under a preheated hot grill or on a barbecue grill for 3-5 minutes each side or until polenta is golden and vegetables are brown and tender.*
4 *To serve, top polenta triangles with rocket, grilled vegetables, pesto and Parmesan cheese shavings.*

Note: *When grilling or barbecuing polenta as in this recipe it is important that the polenta is placed on the preheated surface and left alone until a crust forms. Once the crust forms completely the polenta can easily be turned. Do not be tempted to try turning it too soon or the delicious crust will be left on the grill.*

Serves 8

ingredients

8 cups/2 litres/3 1/2 pt water
2 cups/350g/11oz corn meal (polenta)
125g/4oz butter, chopped
1 tablespoon crushed black peppercorns
125g/4oz grated Parmesan cheese
2 tablespoons olive oil
2 zucchini (courgettes), cut into strips
1 red pepper, cut into thin strips
1 eggplant (aubergine), cut into strips
125g/4oz rocket leaves
1/2 cup/125g/4oz ready-made pesto
fresh Parmesan cheese shavings

vegetable skewers with tahini

Method:

1. *Thread zucchini (courgettes), red and yellow or green peppers, squash and feta cheese onto lightly oiled skewers. Brush skewers with oil and cook on a preheated hot barbecue or under a hot grill for 2 minutes each side or until brown and vegetables are tender crisp.*
2. *To make dip, place tahini, yoghurt, lime juice, chilli sauce, tomato paste (purée) and black pepper to taste in a bowl and mix to combine. Serve with kebabs.*

   Note: *When threading the vegetables onto the skewers make sure that the vegetables have a flat outside surface – this will make them easier to grill.*

   Tahini is a thick oily paste made from crushed toasted sesame seeds. On standing the oil tends to separate out and before using it is necessary to beat it back into the paste. It is available from Middle Eastern food and health food stores and most supermarkets.

   Serves 4

ingredients

3 zucchini (courgettes), cut into 2cm/3/4in cubes
2 red peppers, cut into 2cm/3/4in cubes
2 yellow or green peppers, cut into 2cm/3/4in cubes
8 patty pan squash, halved
185 g/6 oz feta cheese, cut into 2cm/3/4in cubes
2 tablespoons chilli oil

Tahini dip
1/2 cup/125g/4oz tahini
3 tablespoons thick natural yoghurt
2 tablespoons lime juice
1 tablespoon sweet chilli sauce
1 tablespoon tomato paste (purée)
freshly ground black pepper

barbecue
secrets

No barbecue book would be complete without a section on the extras that seem to make everyone else's barbecue a raging success. In this chapter you will find many secrets for perfect barbecuing.

Savoury Butters

Savoury butters are a great way to add taste after cooking – place a piece on a steak or in a baked potato. Garlic butter is probably the best known, but you can make a variety of tasty butters.

To make a parsley butter, place 125 g/4 oz softened butter, a dash of lemon juice, 1 tablespoon finely chopped fresh parsley and pepper to taste in a food processor or blender and process to combine. Shape butter into a log, wrap in plastic food wrap and refrigerate until firm.

This is the basic recipe for a savoury butter and the parsley can be replaced with any flavouring of your choice. Any fresh herbs can be used in place of the parsley – you might like to try chives, rosemary, thyme or basil. Combining different herbs can create an interesting flavour. Other delicious flavours are horseradish, anchovy, roasted red or green pepper, curry paste, mustard, onion, spring onions, capers, finely grated lemon or lime rind.

Barbecue sauce

1 tablespoon vegetable oil
1 onion, chopped
1 clove garlic, crushed
1 teaspoon mustard powder
1 tablespoon Worcestershire sauce
1 tablespoon brown sugar
3 tablespoons tomato sauce
1 teaspoon chilli sauce
3/4 cup/185mL/6fl oz beef stock
freshly ground black pepper

Heat oil in a saucepan and cook onion and garlic for 3-4 minutes or until soft. Stir in mustard powder, Worcestershire sauce, sugar, tomato sauce, chilli sauce and stock. Bring to the boil, then reduce heat and simmer for 8-10 minutes or until sauce reduces and thickens slightly. Season to taste with black pepper.

Makes 1 cup/250 mL/8 fl oz

Mexican chilli sauce

Wonderful with steak, chops or sausages, this sauce will spice up any meal.

2 tablespoons vegetable oil
2 small fresh red chillies, seeded and finely chopped
3 small fresh green chillies, seeded and finely chopped
3 cloves garlic, crushed
2 onions, finely chopped
1 tablespoon finely chopped fresh coriander
440g/14oz canned tomatoes, undrained and mashed
1 teaspoon brown sugar

1/2 teaspoon ground cinnamon
1/4 teaspoon ground cloves
1/4 teaspoon ground ginger
2 tablespoons lemon juice
3 tablespoons water

Heat oil in a frying pan and cook red and green chillies, garlic, onions and coriander for 2-3 minutes. Stir in tomatoes, sugar, cinnamon, cloves, ginger, lemon juice and water. Bring to the boil, then reduce heat and simmer for 15-20 minutes or until sauce reduces and thickens.

Makes 2 cups/500 mL/16 fl oz

Sweet and sour barbecue sauce

A sweet and sour sauce is always a popular accompaniment for chicken and pork, but is also delicious served with sausages and fish.

1 tablespoon vegetable oil
1 small onion, chopped
1 red pepper, chopped
1 tablespoon soy sauce
2 tablespoons honey
1 tablespoon tomato paste (purée)
2 tablespoons cornflour
1/2 cup/125mL/4fl oz cider vinegar
1/2 cup/125mL/4fl oz chicken stock or water
440g/14oz canned pineapple pieces, drained

1. *Heat oil in a saucepan and cook onion and red pepper for 4-5 minutes or until soft. Place soy sauce, honey, tomato paste (purée), cornflour and vinegar in a bowl and mix to combine.*
2. *Stir cornflour mixture into vegetables, then stir in stock or water. Cook, stirring, over a medium heat for 2-3 minutes or until sauce boils and thickens. Stir in pineapple pieces and cook for 2-3 minutes longer.*

Makes 2 cups/500 mL/16 fl oz

Apple and horseradish sauce

Delicious served with beef and sausages, this condiment also makes an interesting accompaniment for barbecued fish.

1/2 cup/125mL/4fl oz cream (double)
1 green apple, cored and grated
3 tablespoons horseradish relish
freshly ground black pepper

Place cream in a bowl and whip until soft peaks form. Fold in apple and horseradish relish and season to taste with black pepper.

Makes 1 cup/250 mL/8 fl oz

barbecue
secrets

What's in a marinade

A marinade tenderises the tough, moistens the dry and flavours the bland. It can be that secret ingredient that turns an otherwise ordinary piece of meat, fish, poultry or game into a taste sensation.

A marinade consists of an acid ingredient, an oil and flavourings – each ingredient playing an important role in the marinating process.

The acid ingredient:

This can be lemon or lime juice, vinegar, wine, soy sauce, yogurt or tomatoes. The acid in a marinade tenderises foods such as beef, lamb, pork, poultry and seafood.

The oil:

The moisturiser in the marinade. Olive and vegetable oils are the most popular but nut, herb or seed oils can also add an interesting flavour. A rule of thumb is that a marinade for barbecuing or grilling should contain at least 25 per cent oil, so each 1 cup/250mL/8fl oz of marinade, should include 1/4 cup/60mL/2fl oz oil.

The flavourings:

Most commonly these are fresh or dried herbs and spices, garlic, ginger or onions.

How to marinate:

As marinades contain acid ingredients, the food and marinade should be placed in stainless steel, enamel, glass or ceramic dishes. The marinade should come up around the sides of the food, but need not completely cover it. Turn the food several times during marinating. Food can also be marinated in a plastic food bag. This is particularly good for marinating large pieces of meat such as roasts. Place the food and marinade in the bag, squeeze out as much air as possible and seal with a rubber band or tie with a piece of string. Turn the bag several times during marinating.

How long to marinate:

Marinating times can be anywhere between 15 minutes and 2 days. As a general rule, the longer you marinate the more tender and flavoursome the food will be. Food marinates faster at room temperature than in the refrigerator. But remember, in hot weather it is usually better to allow a longer marinating time in the refrigerator to ensure that the food stays safe to eat. Fish and seafood should not be marinated for longer than 30 minutes, as the acid ingredient in the marinade will 'cook' the fish. If marinating in the refrigerator, allow the food to stand at room temperature for 30 minutes before cooking to ensure even cooking of the marinated food.

Cooking marinated food:

Drain the food well before cooking, especially when cooking in a frying pan or on a barbecue plate (griddle). Wet food will stew rather than brown. The remaining marinade can be brushed over the food several times during cooking.

Coffee honey marinade

This delicious no-salt-added marinade is excellent for beef and lamb.

1 tablespoon honey
1 tablespoon instant coffee powder
1/4 cup/60 mL/2 fl oz lemon juice
2 cloves garlic, crushed

1. *Place honey, coffee powder, lemon juice and garlic in a small bowl and mix to combine.*
2. *Pour marinade over meat, cover and set aside to marinate.*

White wine and herb marinade

This tasty marinade is ideal for fish and poultry. Choose the herbs that you like or that are in season.

3/4 cup/185 mL/6fl oz white wine
1/4 cup/60 mL/2 fl oz olive oil
2 spring onions, finely chopped
1 tablespoon chopped fresh herbs, or 1 teaspoon dried herbs

1. *Place wine, oil, spring onions and herbs in a bowl and mix to combine.*
2. *Pour marinade over poultry or fish, cover and set aside to marinate.*

Red wine marinade

An excellent marinade for any type of red meat or game. For lighter meat, such as lamb, choose a lighter red wine – for example a Pinot Noir – while for game you can use a heavier red wine such as a Hermitage.

1 1/2 cups/375mL/12fl oz red wine
1/2 cup/125mL/4fl oz olive oil
1 small onion, diced
1 bay leaf, torn into pieces
1 teaspoon black peppercorns, cracked
1 clove garlic, crushed
3 teaspoons finely chopped fresh thyme or 1 teaspoon dried thyme

1. *Place wine, oil, onion, bay leaf, peppercorns, garlic and thyme in a small bowl and mix to combine.*
2. *Pour marinade over meat, cover and set aside to marinate.*

Lemon herb marinade

1/2 cup/125 mL/4fl oz olive oil
1/4 cup/60 mL/2fl oz lemon juice
1/4 cup/60 mL/2fl oz white wine vinegar
1 clove garlic, crushed
1 teaspoon finely grated lemon rind
2 teaspoons finely chopped fresh parsley
2 teaspoons snipped fresh chives
3 teaspoons finely chopped fresh rosemary or 1 teaspoon finely chopped dried rosemary

1. *Place oil, lemon juice, vinegar, garlic, lemon rind, parsley, chives and rosemary in a small bowl and mix to combine.*
2. *Pour marinade over meat or poultry, cover and set aside to marinate.*

Hot chilli marinade

1/4 cup/60 mL/2fl oz soy sauce
1/4 cup/60 mL/2fl oz hoisin sauce
1/2 cup/125 mL/4fl oz dry sherry
1 clove garlic, crushed
1 teaspoon grated fresh ginger
2 spring onions, finely chopped
1 teaspoon hot chilli sauce

1. *Place soy sauce, hoisin sauce, sherry, garlic, ginger, spring onions and chilli sauce in a small bowl and mix to combine.*
2. *Pour marinade over meat or poultry, cover and set aside to marinate. Use the marinade as a baste when barbecuing.*

Cooking is not an exact science: one does not require finely calibrated scales, pipettes and scientific equipment to cook, yet the conversion to metric measures in some countries and its interpretations must have intimidated many a good cook.

Weights are given in the recipes only for ingredients such as meats, fish, poultry and some vegetables. Though a few grams/ounces one way or another will not affect the success of your dish.

Though recipes have been tested using the Australian Standard 250mL cup, 20mL tablespoon and 5mL teaspoon, they will work just as well with the US and Canadian 8fl oz cup, or the UK 300mL cup. We have used graduated cup measures in preference to tablespoon measures so that proportions are always the same. Where tablespoon measures have been given, these are not crucial measures, so using the smaller tablespoon of the US or UK will not affect the recipe's success. At least we all agree on the teaspoon size.

For breads, cakes and pastries, the only area which might cause concern is where eggs are used, as proportions will then vary. If working with a 250mL or 300mL cup, use large eggs (60g/2oz), adding a little more liquid to the recipe for 300mL cup measures if it seems necessary. Use the medium-sized eggs (55g/1¼oz) with 8fl oz cup measure. A graduated set of measuring cups and spoons is recommended, the cups in particular for measuring dry ingredients. Remember to level such ingredients to ensure their accuracy.

English measures

All measurements are similar to Australian with two exceptions: the English cup measures 300mL/10fl oz, whereas the Australian cup measure 250mL/8fl oz. The English tablespoon (the Australian dessertspoon) measures 14.8mL/½fl oz against the Australian tablespoon of 20mL/¾fl oz.

American measures

The American reputed pint is 16fl oz, a quart is equal to 32fl oz and the American gallon, 128fl oz. The Imperial measurement is 20fl oz to the pint, 40fl oz a quart and 160fl oz one gallon.

The American tablespoon is equal to 14.8mL/½fl oz, the teaspoon is 5mL/⅙fl oz. The cup measure is 250mL/8fl oz, the same as Australia.

Dry measures

All the measures are level, so when you have filled a cup or spoon, level it off with the edge of a knife. The scale below is the "cook's equivalent"; it is not an exact conversion of metric to imperial measurement. To calculate the exact metric equivalent yourself, use 2.2046 lb = 1kg or 1 lb = 0.45359kg

Metric		Imperial	
g = grams		oz = ounces	
kg = kilograms		lb = pound	
15g		½oz	
20g		⅔oz	
30g		1oz	
60g		2oz	
90g		3oz	
125g		4oz	¼ lb
155g		5oz	
185g		6oz	
220g		7oz	
250g		8oz	½ lb
280g		9oz	
315g		10oz	
345g		11oz	
375g		12oz	¾ lb
410g		13oz	
440g		14oz	
470g		15oz	
1,000g	1kg	35.2oz	2.2 lb
	1.5kg		3.3 lb

Oven temperatures

The Celsius temperatures given here are not exact; they have been rounded off and are given as a guide only. Follow the manufacturer's temperature guide, relating it to oven description given in the recipe. Remember gas ovens are hottest at the top, electric ovens at the bottom and convection-fan forced ovens are usually even throughout. We included Regulo numbers for gas cookers which may assist. To convert °C to °F multiply °C by 9 and divide by 5 then add 32.

Oven temperatures

	C°	F°	Regulo
Very slow	120	250	1
Slow	150	300	2
Moderately slow	150	325	3
Moderate	180	350	4
Moderately hot	190-200	370-400	5-6
Hot	210-220	410-440	6-7
Very hot	230	450	8
Super hot	250-290	475-500	9-10

Cake dish sizes

Metric	Imperial
15cm	6in
18cm	7in
20cm	8in
23cm	9in

Loaf dish sizes

Metric	Imperial
23x12cm	9x5in
25x8cm	10x3in
28x18cm	11x7in

Liquid measures

Metric	Imperial	Cup & Spoon
mL	fl oz	
millilitres	fluid ounce	
5mL	1/6fl oz	1 teaspoon
20mL	2/3fl oz	1 tablespoon
30mL	1fl oz	1 tablespoon plus 2 teaspoons
60mL	2fl oz	1/4 cup
85mL	2 1/2fl oz	1/3 cup
100mL	3fl oz	3/8 cup
125mL	4fl oz	1/2 cup
150mL	5fl oz	1/4 pint, 1 gill
250mL	8fl oz	1 cup
300mL	10fl oz	1/2 pint)
360mL	12fl oz	1 1/2 cups
420mL	14fl oz	1 3/4 cups
500mL	16fl oz	2 cups
600mL	20fl oz 1 pint,	2 1/2 cups
1 litre	35fl oz 1 3/4 pints,	4 cups

Cup measurements

One cup is equal to the following weights.

	Metric	Imperial
Almonds, flaked	90g	3oz
Almonds, slivered, ground	125g	4oz
Almonds, kernel	155g	5oz
Apples, dried, chopped	125g	4oz
Apricots, dried, chopped	190g	6oz
Breadcrumbs, packet	125g	4oz
Breadcrumbs, soft	60g	2oz
Cheese, grated	125g	4oz
Choc bits	155g	5oz
Coconut, desiccated	90g	3oz
Cornflakes	30g	1oz
Currants	155g	5oz
Flour	125g	4oz
Fruit, dried (mixed, sultanas etc)	185g	6oz
Ginger, crystallised, glace	250g	8oz
Honey, treacle, golden syrup	315g	10oz
Mixed peel	220g	7oz
Nuts, chopped	125g	4oz
Prunes, chopped	220g	7oz
Rice, cooked	155g	5oz
Rice, uncooked	220g	7oz
Rolled oats	90g	3oz
Sesame seeds	125g	4oz
Shortening (butter, margarine)	250g	8oz
Sugar, brown	155g	5oz
Sugar, granulated or caster	250g	8oz
Sugar, sifted icing	155g	5oz
Wheatgerm	60g	2oz

Length

Some of us still have trouble converting imperial length to metric. In this scale, measures have been rounded off to the easiest-to-use and most acceptable figures.
To obtain the exact metric equivalent in converting inches to centimetres, multiply inches by 2.54 whereby 1 inch equals 25.4 millimetres and 1 millimetre equals 0.03937 inches.

Metric	Imperial
mm=millimetres	in = inches
cm=centimetres	ft = feet
5mm, 0.5cm	1/4in
10mm, 1.0cm	1/2in
20mm, 2.0cm	3/4in
2.5cm	1in
5cm	2in
8cm	3in
10cm	4in
12cm	5in
15cm	6in
18cm	7in
20cm	8in
23cm	9in
25cm	10in
28cm	11in
30cm	1 ft, 12in

index

STEP-BY-STEP

INDIAN COOKING

SHARDA GOPAL

with Introductory text by Linda Sonntag

NEW BURLINGTON BOOKS

This book is dedicated to my late father and mother, my husband, my daughter Suji and my son Sonny.

A Quarto Book

This edition Published in 1989 by
New Burlington Books
6 Blundell Street
London N7 9BH

British Library Cataloguing in Publication Data
Gopal, Sharda
Step-by-step Indian cooking.
1. Cooking, India
I. Title
641.5954 TX724.5.14
ISBN 1 85348 211 0

This book was designed and produced by
Quarto Publishing plc
The Old Brewery
6 Blundell Street
London N7 9BH

Senior Editor: Polly Powell
Editor: Linda Sonntag

Designer: Michael Morey
Art Editor: Moira Clinch

Photographers: Trevor Wood and Michael Bull
Home Economist: Veronica Bull

Art Director: Pete Laws
Editorial Director: Jim Miles

Thanks to Vincent T. Murphy, Paul Gardner and Adrian Saunders

Typeset by Facsimile Graphics Ltd
Coggeshall, Essex

Manufactured in Hong Kong by Regent Publishing Services Limited
Printed by Lee Fung Asco Printers Limited
Hong Kong

Quarto Publishing would like to take this opportunity to thank Pat Chapman and The Curry Club, PO Box 7, Haslemere, Surrey.
Thanks are also due to Elizabeth Parkinson and the Red Fort Restaurant, and to Suji Gopal.

Contents

Foreword

More and more people in the West are being introduced to the exotic tastes of Indian food as Indian restaurants mushroom in the high streets of nearly every major western city, and many people have been inspired to try and cook Indian dishes in their own kitchens. However, traditionally, the knowledge and skills of Indian cooking have been handed down in the family from mother to daughter, and are learnt from practical experience. In this way, I learnt to cook from my mother. I hope that this book will unravel the mysteries of Indian cooking for those not brought up in the Indian tradition, and make Indian cuisine accessible to even the most amateur cook.

Having been brought up in the Kerala region of southern India, and having lived in both western and northern India, I have been lucky enough to supplement my inherited knowledge with recipes and techniques gleaned from many of the culturally different areas of India. This varied experience and understanding of regional variations has helped me to present this unique collection of recipes. Although the use of spices in the recipes is relatively minimal, it is the subtle combination of these spices and the selection of aromatics that make the dishes in this book different from those that you might find ordinarily in other Indian cookery books or restaurants.

Needless to say, the best Indian food is to be found in Indian homes. All the dishes in this book are those that I give to my family and friends, and I hope that you enjoy making them as much as I have.

Sharda Gopal

SHARDA GOPAL

INTRODUCTION

India is a land of spectacular contrasts, from the emerald Vale of Kashmir in the snow-clad mountains of the north to the steaming jungles and palm-fringed beaches of the tropical south. Across this vast country of 700 million inhabitants the intricate use of spices unites all the kitchens of the land into producing food that is uniquely Indian.

There are about 25 spices on the shelf in the Indian pantry. Many of them will have come from the back garden along with fresh herbs and bulbs — onions, garlic and shallots. With this huge treasury of flavours the Indian cook can create an infinite number of different dishes. Spices can be used individually or combined, roasted or ground with water into a paste to produce flavours anywhere in the spectrum from sweet to sour, fiery to bland and fragrant to pungent.

Indians are almost intuitively aware of the medicinal properties of the herbs and spices they use to flavour their food, and they eat not just for sheer enjoyment and to stay alive, but to keep their bodies healthy and well-tuned. Apart from their medicinal properties, spices and other condiments can be used to offset the extremes of temperature. In the north, warming spices take the bite out of freezing winter days, and in the south bitter-sweet tamarind has a soothing effect in the airless midday heat.

ABOVE *Based on Chinese design, this cantilevered fishing net is large enough to catch sufficient fish to feed an entire village with a hearty meal.*

ABOVE *The palm groves of Kerala in southern India provide plenty of coconuts, an essential ingredient of many local dishes.*

Of course what is eaten also depends largely on local produce. Broadly speaking, bread is eaten in the north and rice in the south. In the south the food tends to be more fiery (and paradoxically more refreshing, even if it does bring tears to the eyes). In Kerala, in particular, grow the coconut palms, the tamarind and jackfruit trees and the spice gardens that made Cochin rich and famous.

In the south, the tropical heat is put to use to mature pickles and for overnight fermentation of bread and cakes made from ground peas without the addition of yeast. Southerners often steam their food, whereas in the north it is oven-cooked. In Rajasthan in the northwest, picnickers make an impromptu oven by digging a pit for a cow-dung fire on which they will cook spiced meat in a clay pot. The lid of the pot is sealed with dough, and more burning dung is heaped over it. This technique is called 'dum' — food is baked slowly all the way through and all the juices are kept in, resulting in the tenderest meat and the richest possible flavour.

In Kashmir the winters are made bearable by cooking with warming spices, particularly cinnamon. People carry around baskets of live charcoal to keep the cold at bay between meals, and these baskets serve a double purpose, often baking an egg or a potato for a hot snack.

Kashmir is a land of lakes and tranquil water gardens. The lakes produce abundant fish and delicious lotus roots. Ingenious farmers make floating vegetable gardens from reeds and mud, which can be towed about or left to drift picturesquely at anchor. When they are harvested, vegetables are sold from boats at the floating market. As autumn draws in there is a frenzy of mushroom picking and all kinds of vegetables, especially chillies, are hung up on the rafters to dry to keep the family supplied when the snows come. To see them through the winter, the Kashmiris make a dried spice cake called *ver*, crushing their spices according to a family recipe, then mixing them to a paste with mustard oil. The cake is hung up and bits are broken off it as required.

In the east, the Bengalis are noted for their love of fish and their insatiable desire for sweets, especially jaggery (raw sugar). Sugar cane is pressed to extract the juice, which is then heated over wood fires and patiently stirred for many hours until it is thick enough to set. Lumps of it are eaten as sweets and the Bengalis are so fond of it that they even manage to

FAR LEFT AND LEFT *From the exuberance of the Palace of the Four Winds at Jaipur to the simplicity of the local post office, India is a sub-continent with many architectural delights.*

LEFT AND ABOVE *For most of the time the elephant is a humble beast of burden, earning its keep by carrying and pulling heavy loads but on festive occasions is profusely decorated and becomes the centre of much attention.*

ABOVE *Nuts are used in both savoury and sweet Indian recipes. This nut vendor is a well-known figure outside the Amber Palace in Rajastan.*

RIGHT *Sweet stalls are a common sight on the streets of Indian cities, particularly in western regions. Made from liquid sugar, many varieties are unimaginably sweet to the Western palate.*

ABOVE OPPOSITE *Indians are intuitively aware of the medicinal properties of certain foods and the medicine man's stall will often display herbs and spices also available from food stalls.*

slip it into their vegetable curries.

Bombay in Maharashtra on the west coast, India's Hollywood and boom town founded on seven islands, has its own sweet treats — biscuits made of rice flour. They take several days and many processes to make, and are served at religious festivals.

Lucknow in Uttar Pradesh glories in whole chickens stuffed with quails, and a celebration halva made from the yolks of 100 eggs. Another local extravagance is a pearl pilaf — a dish of rice and 'pearls' made by stuffing a chicken's oesophagus with a mixture of egg yolks and real gold and silver, and tying it at intervals to resemble a string of pearls. It is then boiled and slit open, and the 'pearls' pop out, looking very like the real thing.

All over India, the laws of religion rule what is eaten. Hindus are vegetarian, although the priestly caste of Kashmiri Brahmins do eat meat, abstaining instead from cooking with garlic and onions, which they believe inflame the passions. Jains are such strict vegetarians that they will neither eat root vegetables, for fear of killing insects as they dig, nor will they touch tomatoes or aubergines, whose colour reminds them of blood. The Muslims will not eat pork and nowhere except in the state of Kerala is it permitted to kill the sacred cow. One sect of Muslims, the Bohris, alternate salt and sweet dishes and begin their meal by eating a pinch of salt in praise of Allah.

Presenting the meal

The traditional way to serve Indian food is on a thali or large tray, often of beautifully wrought metal. Each different dish will be in a small metal or earthenware bowl perched around the edge of the tray, or laid out on a low communal brass table. The diners sit on the floor, or on very low stools. The carpet is spread with coloured cloth to protect it and the guests are given giant coloured napkins. The dishes can be wrapped in cotton or silk, which is loosely folded back over the food after it has been served. Often banana leaves will serve as disposable plates. More people today are sitting up to a table with chairs, although in many parts the men are still served first, and then the women eat together on the floor in the kitchen.

Indians eat with their hands. The right hand only is used — the left is thought unclean. In some parts of India the whole hand is used; in others just the fingertips. Generally, food is scooped up with a piece of flat bread in the north and mopped up with rice in the south. It means that cleanliness is very important — hands are washed before and after eating and water for washing is provided even on barrows selling snacks in the streets.

In all parts of India hospitality is legendary. All the dishes, including fruit and sweetmeats, are offered at once. Decoration is simple (nuts, chopped herbs, lemon slices) and sometimes exotic — silver and gold leaf *vark* on special occasions provide a direct, although expensive, source of minerals.

Cold water is drunk with meals. Breakfast, which might be a sweet flaky bread in the foothills of the Himalayas, a potato curry in the capital, Delhi, or a steamed bean cake *(idli)* in the south, is served with tea, sometimes spiced with cinnamon, or with hot strong coffee. During the day an Indian might drink freshly pressed fruit juice (mango is the favourite), coconut milk (in the south), or *lassi*, a sweet and sometimes salty drink made from yoghurt. Muslims are forbidden alcohol, but there is plenty of potent liquor about for those who want it. Other drinks include *Asha* which is distilled from jaggery, palm toddy and, of course, gin.

After a meal the hostess may offer betel leaves — glossy green leaves with mildly anaesthetic properties and a refreshing taste. These are chewed and then spat out (or more delicately removed), like gum. They can be taken neat or wrapped around nuts, quicklime, cardamon pods, cloves or tobacco. Shah Jahan, one of India's more colourful rulers and the builder of the Taj Mahal, was even known to wrap them around poison for his less-welcome guests.

Mr and Mrs Gopal, who now live in England, have travelled all over India. From the north they collected enticing meat dishes; from the east, characteristic fish delicacies. The vegetable dishes originate mainly in the south and west. From the south, too, comes their love of coconut, hot spicy vegetable dishes and lentils. This is an individual collection of recipes: the flavour is wholly Indian.

Presentation is an important part of good Indian cooking, and imaginative use of garnishes can make an ordinary dish into something really special. Tomatoes, lettuce and coriander leaves are often used to add colour and a crisp texture to savoury dishes.

TOP LEFT *Red Peppers Stuffed with Vegetables,* CENTRE LEFT *Sardines in a Thick Spicy Sauce,* BELOW LEFT *Baked Fish Stuffed with Mushrooms,* TOP RIGHT *Vegetable Curry, Kerala Style,* CENTRE RIGHT *Yellow Rice with Hard-Boiled Eggs,* BELOW RIGHT *Pumpkin Halva.*

Section One

THE INDIAN KITCHEN

BASIC TECHNIQUES AND TIPS

In India every kitchen was traditionally equipped (and many still are) with a grinding stone — a large flat stone placed on the floor, in front of which the housewife or cook's assistant sat cross-legged, pounding chillies and spices with another stone. An electric blender is obviously the modern equivalent of the grinding stone, and can also be used for puréeing chickpeas etc. A coffee grinder is ideal for making spice pastes. If you are going to buy a blender or grinder with this purpose in mind, it is best to choose one where the blades are as low as possible, as you will be working with small quantities. A pestle and mortar is still the best bet for very small quantities of hard seeds. Both pestle and mortar should be made of marble, if possible. This will make it quite an expensive item to buy, but remember that metal reacts with acids and wood absorbs flavours.

The old-fashioned way of cooking in India is over a charcoal fire, where food can be spit-roasted, or cooked in a heavy pan with hot charcoal heaped on the lid to give an even distribution of heat. The next best thing is a set of cast-iron pans or casseroles that can be used on the top of the stove or in the oven, and which have tightly fitting lids. You can improve the fit of a lid by covering the pan with a sheet of aluminium foil and then putting the lid on top. The advantage of cast-iron pans is that they transmit the heat well and stay hot when removed from the stove. Food tends to stick to glazed enamel, and this is best avoided. A set of asbestos mats will give you even better heat control.

For cooking bread, Indians use a heavy flat pan called a tava. Any flat iron pan will be right for this job, and you can use it for roasting spices too (see below).

Other equipment that you will need will probably be in your kitchen already. Most essential is a set of good sharp knives for trimming meat and cutting up vegetables. Then you will need a sieve, a colander, a grater with various blades that will tackle anything from a cabbage to a nutmeg, wooden spoons, skewers and a square of muslin.

As there are often a lot of ingredients in a recipe, it is a good idea to measure them out and have them ready before you begin to cook, so that you are not held up looking for things at a crucial moment.

Peeling tomatoes

Many of the recipes call for peeled tomatoes. You can use tinned tomatoes to save time, and in winter, but fresh ripe tomatoes are best. Drop them into a bowl of boiling water and leave for a minute or two until a split appears in the skin. Drain and refresh in cold water. The skin can then be removed quite easily.

Adding yoghurt

This procedure has to be done carefully or the yoghurt will separate. Take the pan from the heat and add the yoghurt a spoonful at a time, stirring well between each addition. Then return the pan to the heat, stirring all the time, until the sauce bubbles.

Cooking the spice paste until the oil runs clear

The point of this operation is to allow the spices to absorb as much oil as they can, and thus to give out their full flavour. When the spices are saturated, the excess oil runs out of them (you can drain it off, if you like), and you can proceed to the next step in the recipe.

Grinding spices

A coffee grinder is ideal for making a spice paste. You can also use a blender or a pestle and mortar (see above).

Dropping spices into hot oil

This is often either the first or the last step in an Indian recipe. The oil is heated until very hot and then whole spices or dried chillies are dropped into it. Within a few seconds they pop or expand and their concentrated flavour is released. The oil and spices are then used as the starting point of a recipe, or they are poured over the finished dish.

Roasting spices

Heat a flat cast-iron pan without any fat or oil, add the spices and shake them about until their roasted fragrance emerges. Roasted spices can be cooled and stored or used straight away, either whole or ground.

Thickening sauces

Flour is not used as a thickening agent in Indian cookery. Instead, spice pastes, yoghurt, tomatoes and coconut are all used to thicken and add their own individual flavours.

Clarifying butter to make ghee

You can buy ghee in Indian grocery shops but you can also make it at home. Cut up a block of unsalted butter, put it in a heavy saucepan and melt it over a low flame. Let it bubble gently until solid yellow particles form, strain it through muslin and allow to cool. Ghee does not need to be refrigerated.

Browing onions and garlic

This is essential if you want your curry sauces to have a good strong colour.

Making yoghurt

Yoghurt is expensive to buy and if you use it in large quantities it is worth making yourself. Scald 600ml (1pt) milk, then take it off the heat and allow it to cool to lukewarm. Put 2 tbsp natural yoghurt in a bowl, whisk it and then gradually whisk in the milk. Cover the bowl and leave it in a warm place overnight until the yoghurt has set. Store in the fridge. Keep 2 tbsp yoghurt back to make your next batch.

Squeezing tamarind

Break off 50g (2oz) tamarind from the block and soak it in twice its volume of very hot water for a couple of hours. Now, squeeze the pulp well or press it through a sieve with a wooden spoon to get out all the juice.

Coconuts

You can test the freshness of a coconut by shaking it; if there is plenty of liquid sloshing around inside it, it is fresh. Get the liquid out by punching two holes in the eyes of the coconut. You can drink this liquid (it is very refreshing chilled) but it is not used for cooking in this book. Now give the coconut a good whack with a hammer to open it. Use a knife to prise the flesh from the shell. If this is difficult, put the coconut pieces shell-side-down over a low flame for a minute or two. The shell will contract and release the flesh. (Alternatively, you can put the coconut in a warm oven for 15 minutes before you crack it.) Peel the brown skin off the white flesh with a potato peeler. Grate the coconut by hand or in a food processor.

If you want to extract the coconut milk for cooking, put the grated coconut in a blender with enough hot water to make it easy for the blades to turn. Strain the mixture through muslin and squeeze out all the liquid. Put the squeezed coconut back in the blender and repeat the process with more hot water. Some recipes call for the milk from the first and second pressings to be used at different stages, so you should, of course, strain them into separate bowls. (The first milk will be much thicker.)

SPICES AND AROMATICS IN THE INDIAN KITCHEN

Spices and aromatics are the very heart of Indian cooking. Flowers, leaves, roots, bark, seeds and bulbs (the simplest of natural ingredients) are used in endless combinations to produce an infinite variety of flavours: sweet, sharp, hot, sour, spicy, aromatic, tart, mild, fragrant or pungent.

The Indian cook aims to create blends of spices so subtle that a completely new taste arises — something indefinable. Sometimes the flavour of one particular spice can be magnified by the careful underplay of several others. As many as 15 spices may be used in one dish, or there might be only one. Spices, unlike herbs, can be used together without loss of flavour.

It is best to buy your spices whole and to grind them at home (see page 18) if the recipe call for it. Whole spices keep longer than spice powders, which quickly lose their aroma. But even whole spices begin to taste tired after a while so buy small quantities and keep them in airtight jars in a cool dark place. Do not buy curry powder — this is a blanket term for a blend of inferior spices and will make everything taste the same.

Asafoetida *(Hing)*
This is a resin and comes from Kashmir. It is bought ground and is said to smell of truffles. The flavour is quite pungent, but it is used mainly for its digestive properties, especially in the cooking of beans, where it combats flatulence. A pinch of it can be fried in hot oil before the rest of the ingredients are cooked.

Biriyani masala
This is a special sweet spice mix for biriyani dishes. Grind together the cardamom seeds from 8 pods, 25g (1oz) cinnamon stick, 6 cloves and 1 tsp fennel seeds.

Cardamom *(Elaichi)*
Pale green cardamom pods contain tiny black seeds and grow in the rain forests of southern India. They have a sweet fragrant flavour and can be used whole (although the pod is not usually eaten) or the seeds can be taken out of the pods and used separately. This is a fiddly business, but seeds are not usually sold out of their pods because they lose their flavour too fast. Some recipes use ground cardamom seeds and as they are so small, it is best to grind them with a pestle and mortar.

Cayenne pepper *(Pisi hui lal mirch)*
Cayenne pepper, like paprika, comes from the seeds of plants in the capsicum family. It is a blend of various types of chilli powder. The capsicum family is large, ranging from the sweet pepper to the chilli. In general, the smaller the fruit, the hotter it is. Cayenne is sold as a powder. It should not be as hot as chilli powder, but it is pretty hot and should therefore be used with care.

Chilli *(Mirchi)*
Chilli is the hottest flavour on earth. Chillies and chilli powder should be used with extreme care. Do not take a bite or even lick one to see how its tastes as the effect will be quite devastating. Also, do not touch your mouth or eyes while handling chillies — the burning will be intense. Whole chillies can be seeded to make them a little less hot. Regulate the quantity of chilli recommended in the recipes according to how much you can bear, and do not forget to tell your guests if you have left a whole chilli lurking in the curry.

You can now buy fresh green chillies at many grocery shops and supermarkets. If you live a long way from a regular supplier of chillies, buy them when you see them, wash them, dry them, put them in a jar and fill it to the brim with oil. Screw the lid on tightly and keep them in a cook dark place. This is a very good way of storing them, and you get a flavoured oil out of it too. Otherwise chillies go mouldy quite quickly. If one is mouldy, all the others will be infected too and the whole lot should be thrown away.

Chillies go red as they ripen, so dried chillies are always red. They are dropped into hot oil to release their aroma before other ingredients are added.

Chilli powder is very hot indeed because it is made from the crushed seeds of the chilli, its hottest part. A blend of chilli, garlic, cumin and oregano is also sold as chilli powder.

Cinnamon *(Dalchini)*
Cinnamon has a rich warm flavour. It is available as a powder but is much better bought in sticks. You can then break off a piece and add it to the curry. It should be discarded before serving. A lot of cinnamon is grown in Sri Lanka and it is the inner bark of a tree related to the laurel. The outer bark is scraped off and the inner bark peeled off in strips and rolled into sticks, which are then dried.

Cloves *(Luong)*
Cloves are the flower buds of an evergreen of the myrtle family. They have been used in India for thousands of years, not only in cookery, but to sweeten the breath and to relieve the pain of toothache. They contain a mild anaesthetic. Cloves are best bought whole and ground, if necessary, at home with a pestle and mortar. Whole cloves are not eaten, but left on the side of the plate.

Coconut *(Nariel)*
Fresh coconut may be grated and frozen. You can buy desiccated coconut in packets in Indian shops or supermarkets, and this can be used if the fresh variety is not available. (For how to prepare a coconut, see page 19.)

Coriander *(Daniya)*
The English name for this spice comes for the Greek *koros,* meaning 'bug'. They are small ridged seeds, light brown in colour and can be easily squashed under the thumb. They are used powdered or whole.

Fresh green coriander *(Hari daniya)*
The leaves of the coriander plant are rather like those of flat-leaved parsley, but darker and more brilliant. Fresh coriander can be quite expensive to buy, but is it just as easily grown as parsley and can be used in the same way, on English as well as Indian dishes. The leaves have a very distictive bitter-sweet taste. The best way of keeping this herb is in a jug of water in the fridge. Tired leaves can be revived by immersing in cold water for an hour, but do not keep them in water as they will go slimy.

Cumin *(Jeera)*
Cumin seeds are long and slim, similar to caraway seeds, but have a distinctive warm aroma. They are used either whole

or ground, and can be bought ground. However, is it best to buy them whole and grind your own at home, as the ground spice loses its flavour quite quickly. Cumin is often used roasted. Drop the whole seeds into a hot dry pan and cook until the roasted fragrance emerges. Shake the pan to prevent sticking. The seeds can be stored whole, or ground in a coffee grinder and stored or used immediately.

Curry leaves *(Kari pulia or Neem)*
These are small grey-greenish leaves, a bit like bay, and are grown in many Indian gardens. They can be used fresh or dried; the dried ones can be crumbled onto food, and their aroma is released by its heat and moisture. They are sometimes fried in the oil the food is cooked in, and then discarded. They can also be eaten.

Food colourings
Turmeric and saffron will colour food yellow, but you can also buy a vegetable colouring that has no taste. Red food colouring is used on tandoori chicken.

Fennel *(Soonf)*
Small oval seeds, greenish and with an anise flavour, they have digestive properties, and are sometimes served roasted at the end of an Indian meal. Used sparingly, they give warmth and sweetness to curries.

Fenugreek *(Methi)*
These tawny coloured seeds are chunky and very hard. Their bitter taste and aroma is released only by cooking. In powdered form, fenugreek is one of the main ingredients of curry powders. It is used sparingly on its own. The leaves of the plant, which is related to spinach, are used in India as a herb.

Garam masala
Garam masala, meaning 'hot spices', is a mixture of ground spices that is used sparingly, sprinkled either on a finished dish or onto the food just before it has finished cooking. It is far better to grind your own spices than to buy the mixture ready-ground. Bought garam masala often contains inferior quality spices and will not keep its flavour for long.

For homemade garam masala, grind together the cardamom seeds from 10 pods, 25g (1oz) cinnamon stick, 6 cloves and 6-8 whole black peppercorns. Store in an airtight jar in a cool place.

Ghee
This is clarified butter and can be made at home (see page 19). The advantage of using ghee is that it can be heated to a very high temperature without burning, and so is useful for browning onions in order to give a sauce a good rich colour, and for sizzling spices before the main ingredients are added to the pan. Because the milk solids have been removed from ghee, it will keep will without being refrigerated. Many people prefer to used unsaturated fats and oils instead of ghee or butter.

Ginger
You can buy ginger ground *(soondth)* or fresh *(adrak).* The ground type is the same as that used in baking. The fresh 'root' ginger is actually a rhizome, and is fawn in colour and knobbly. Inside, the ginger is hard, yellow and fibrous. It is easiest to cook with, once peeled and grated. You can also chop it if you are going to liquidize it with other ingredients. Fresh ginger can be kept wrapped in foil in the freezer or in a pot of sandy soil, kept fairly dry. It has quite a hot pungent flavour and should be used sparingly.

Mango powder *(Amchur)*
Unripe mangoes are sliced and dried, then powdered and sold as amchur. Amchur has a tart taste. If you are unable to find it, use a dash of lemon or lime instead.

Mustard seeds *(Rai)*
There are both white and black mustard seeds — the black contain a higher proportion of the volatile mustard oil. When dropped into hot oil, the mustard seeds pop, releasing their flavour. It is best to put a lid over the pan while you do this, or they will fly all over the kitchen. You can use this technique when shallow-frying Western food to add extra aroma.

Nutmeg and mace *(Jaiphal and Javitri)*
Mace is the fleshy lattice-like covering of the nutmeg, which is golden brown in colour. It is sold whole or powdered. Nutmegs are best bought whole and freshly grated at home.

Oil
Mustard oil, derived from the seeds of the mustard plant, is very popular with south Indian cooks, especially for pickling. This, and coconut oil, can be bought at specialist Indian shops. Coconut oil is stirred together with a little warm water to release its aroma before use.

Groundnut oil, also called arachide oil, is suitable for Indian cooking, as is the oil labelled simply 'vegetable oil'.

Paprika
Paprika is the ground seeds from the capsicum or sweet pepper. It is milder than chilli powder or cayenne.

Peppercorns *(Mirchi)*
Peppercorns grow on large bushes in Malabar, on the west coast of India. They are picked by hand just before they are ripe, when they are still green, then left in the sun to dry and become black and crinkly. White peppercorns are the mature fruit, left to ripen on the bush, with the outer husk removed. This is traditionally done by immersing sacks of peppercorns in running streams. Bacteria get to work and loosen the husks and the water finishes the job. The peppercorns are then trodden in vats, like grapes, to rid them of the final traces of husk.

Black pepper is more aromatic; white pepper is stronger and hotter. Black pepper should always be bought whole and freshly ground over your food as it loses its aroma fast.

Poppy seeds *(Khus-khus)*
It is the milky juice in the poppy's seed pod from which opium is derived — the seeds themselves have no narcotic properties. They are small, black and hard. There is also a white type.

Saffron *(Zaffran)*
Saffron is the most expensive spice of all. It is the filaments from a specially cultivated crocus — 75,000 stamens are needed to make 100g (4oz) of the spice. It is grown in Kashmir and used on festive occasions to give food a bright yellow colour and a distinctive aroma. The filaments can be lightly roasted, crumbled in a little hot water and left to infuse to bring out their full strength. Buy saffron only from a reputable spice

dealer or you may get an adulterated product, or something that is not saffron at all, especially if you buy it ready-powdered.

Sambar powder
This is a delicious aromatic spice mix used in a number of recipes in this book.

100g (4oz) coriander seeds
1 tsp asafoetida
4 whole red chillies
6 curry leaves
25g (1oz) polished split black lentils (urid dal)
25g (1oz) chana dal
25g (1oz) fenugreek seeds
1 tbsp mustard seeds
4-6 whole black peppercorns

Roast together the first four ingredients and set them aside. Then, roast each of the remaining ingredients separately. Some take very little roasting before the fragrance emerges and would burn if roasted with the rest. Now grind all the roasted spices together to a fine powder and store in a screw-topped jar.

Tamarind *(Amli)*
A tamarind looks a little like a cinnamon-coloured pod of broad beans. They grow on tall trees and are peeled and seeded when ripe. The fruit is then squashed into bricks and this is how you buy it. It has a very tart citric flavour and if you cannot find it, use a dash of lemon or lime instead. (For preparing tamarind juice, see page 19.)

Turmeric *(Huldi)*
Turmeric is a rhizome related to ginger. Bought as a powder, it gives curries their characteristic golden yellow colour. It has a delicate taste and is mildly antiseptic, although it becomes bitter if too much is used. Indians often use turmeric with beans because of its digestive properties.

Vindaloo paste
This is a very hot spicy paste. Chillies may be used with their seeds if you like particularly fiery food. In western India

the Christians eat pork vindaloo. For those not permitted pork, vindaloo goes well with beef, lamb or prawns.

10 red chillies
50g (2oz) fresh ginger, finely grated
12 cloves garlic, 4 chopped and 8 thinly sliced
½ tsp fenugreek seeds
1 tsp mustard seeds
1 tsp cumin seeds
2-3 tbsp white wine vinegar
5-6 tbsp oil
225g (8oz) onion, chopped
500g (1lb) tomatoes, peeled
cardamom seeds from 8 pods

Grind or pound the chillies, half of the ginger, chopped garlic, fenugreek, mustard and cumin, and mix them to a paste with the vinegar. Do not add any water. Heat the oil and fry the onion until golden, then add the tomatoes and squash them into a paste as you cook. Stir in the spicy vinegar paste you have already made, add the remaining spices and fry until the oil runs out of them. The paste is then ready. Allow it to cool and store in an airtight container in a cool dark place.

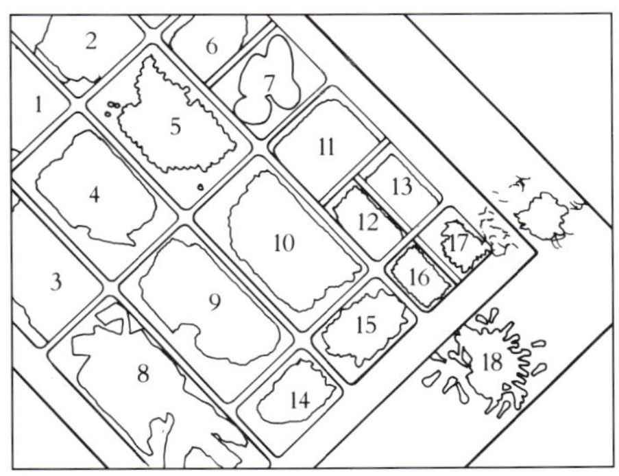

LEFT *Selection of spices.* ***1*** *asafoetida,* ***2*** *garam masala,* ***3*** *turmeric,* ***4*** *ground cinnamon,* ***5*** *black peppercorns,* ***6*** *poppy seeds,* ***7*** *nutmeg,* ***8*** *cassia,* ***9*** *ground ginger,* ***10*** *crushed red chillies,* ***11*** *fenugreek,* ***12*** *cumin,* ***13*** *black mustard seeds,* ***14*** *paprika,* ***15*** *cardamom,* ***16*** *mustard seeds,* ***17*** *saffron,* ***18*** *cloves.*

Typical Menus

A perfectly balanced Indian meal will have dishes that cover a whole range of flavours from mild to hot and from sweet to sour. Texture, too, is considered. There will be dishes that are crunchy, soft, dry, moist, rough and smooth. Some will be served piping hot, while others may be chilled. There might be a meat dish (in the meat-eating households of the north), a fish dish, lentils, rice, two or three vegetable dishes and a salad, several chutneys and a cooling yoghurt. The following are suggestions for menus using recipes from this book, although obviously a meal need not contain more than two or three complementary dishes.

SPICY MENU

Dal Curry 1 (see page 28)

Green Beans Toran 1 (see page 56)

Cauliflower with Potatoes and Tomatoes (see page 69)

Meat Curry with Yoghurt (see page 81)

Prawn Vindaloo (see page 117)

Wholemeal Unleavened Bread (see page 128)

Green Mango Chutney (see page 140)

Beetroot Halva (see page 149)

Prawn Vindaloo is a hot and spicy curry, and this menu would be ideal for those particularly partial to hot dishes. Dal Curry is very nourishing and full of protein, and served in conjunction with dry Green Beans Toran beautifully balances the different and exciting tastes of this meal. Potato and bread provide starch, and can be used to mop up the rich and varied sauces of the other dishes. For those who might find the Vindaloo a little too hot on its own, Green Mango Chutney can be deliciously sweet and soothing. Finally, the Beetroot Halva is an excellent last course, providing coolness and sweetness.

CELEBRATION MENU

Chickpeas with Mango and Coconut (see page 36)

Extra Thick Buttermilk Curry (see page 40)

Lemon Rice (see page 132)

Whole Roast Chicken (see page 105)

Stuffed Okra (see page 61)

Tamarind Chutney (see page 137)

Pineapple Pudding (see page 148)

This is a celebration meal centred around the Whole Roast Chicken, with delicately fragrant Lemon Rice and spicy Stuffed Okra as the main accompaniments. Although this menu would suit those who prefer milder Indian cooking, it nevertheless provides a variety of contrasting and complementary tastes and textures. The Chickpeas with Mango and Coconut is crunchy and blends well with the Buttermilk Curry (a popular Gujarati dish) and the chicken in terms of texture and heat, whereas a good tangy flavour is provided by the chunky Tamarind Chutney.

SAVOURY MENU

Yoghurt Bread (see page 128)

Coconut Chutney (see page 136)

Peanut Soya Sauce (see page 140)

Fried Spiced Meat Keema (see page 85)

Carrot Toran (see page 73)

Yellow Rice with Hard-Boiled Eggs (see page 120)

Melon with Orange Juice (see page 145)

The Punjabis make full use of carrots when they are in season, using them in sweet as well as savoury dishes. In this menu Carrot Toran is a dry spicy dish that not only complements the main dish of Fried Spiced Meat Keema but also adds colour to this tasty spread of Indian cooking.

MEAT & FISH MENU

Green Lentil and Banana Curry (see page 37)

Potato Masala Curry (see page 52)

Mashed Aubergine (see page 60)

Meatball and Cauliflower Curry (see page 89)

Fish Curry with Yoghurt (see page 113)

Vegetable Biriyani (see page 77)

Black Lentil Chutney (see page 141)

Mango Soufflé (see page 149)

Both meat and fish are essential ingredients of this menu and, together with the Vegetable Biriyani, provide a substantial meal. The smooth texture of the Mashed Aubergine effectively offsets the spice and 'bite' of the Potato Masala Curry, and is a soothing dish. Mango Soufflé is both light and fluffy in texture, and is an easily digested conclusion to this satisfying meal.

VEGETARIAN MENU 1

Bitter Gourd with Onion Stuffing (see page 65)

Cauliflower with Coconut Milk (see page 68)

Fried Spiced Prawns (see page 117)

Yellow Rice with Hard-Boiled Eggs (see page 120)

Tomato Salad (see page 144)

Curried Pumpkin and Black-eyed Beans (see page 32)

Steamed Plantain Cake (see page 153)

This is a menu for non-meat eaters; the beans, prawns and eggs provide plenty of protein. The Bitter Gourd with Onion Stuffing is, as its name suggests, a bitter dish and is included for those interested in the more unusual tastes of Indian cooking. In Bengal gourds are served first so that the bitterness cleans the palate in preparation for the main dishes. As this meal is fairly mild, Steamed Plantain Cake is an ideal hot pudding to end the meal.

VEGETARIAN MENU 2

Dal Bread (see page 129)

Vegetable Curry with Roasted Coconut (see page 45)

Green Coriander Chutney (see page 137)

Dry Spiced Potato (see page 49)

Vegetable Curry, Kerala Style (see page 48)

Vegetable Biriyani (see page 77)

Plantain Jaggery (see page 153)

Vegetarians in India rarely eat eggs and get their protein from other ingredients, such as nuts. This menu is for strict vegetarians, containing an enticing assortment of vegetable dishes including one with a rich sauce (Vegetable Curry with Roasted Coconut), one cooked dry (Dry Spiced Potato) and one cooked with rice (Vegetable Biriyani).

Section Two

STEP-BY-STEP RECIPES

PULSES

Dal

India has over 60 varieties of pulses which provide a primary source of protein for her millions of vegetarians. When cooked, they can be left whole or puréed, making them extremely versatile as ingredients for curries, stuffings and patties. They can even be roasted or deep-fried for garnishes or snacks.

To cook pulses, first pick them over and remove any foreign bodies. The larger varieties should be soaked overnight (at least 10 hours). If you are in a hurry, you can bring them to the boil, continue boiling for a couple of minutes and then take the pan off the heat and leave it to stand for an hour before cooking.

Soaked beans are best rinsed to get rid of some of the starch. They will then need to simmer for anything from 15 minutes to over an hour, depending on size and age. Simmer them with the lid slightly open to let the steam escape.

Sometimes beans are simmered with a few of the aromatics that will be used in the curry, but most of them are added at a later stage because of the lengthy cooking time. Ginger and turmeric are favourite flavourings for beans and asafoetida is often added to combat flatulence.

Sprouted pulses are even more nutritious than not-sprouted ones. Sprouted lentils can be bought in packets in some supermarkets and health food shops, but they are expensive. It is cheap and easy to sprout your own lentils at home. Spread them out in a shallow dish and sprinkle them with water or spray them with a plant spray. As soon as the water has been absorbed (after an hour or two), spray them again. Keep them moist for two or three days, and once they have sprouted, they will be ready to eat.

DAL CURRY I

INGREDIENTS (Serves 2)
175g (6oz) toor dal
2 tbsp oil
½ tsp mustard seeds
½ tsp cumin seeds
1 small onion, finely chopped
leaves from 1-2 sprigs coriander
2 tomatoes, peeled and chopped
½ tsp turmeric
1 clove of garlic, finely chopped
2 green chillies, sliced
salt

1 Pick over the dal and wash it well. Bring 850ml (1½pt) water to the boil, add the dal and simmer for about 15 minutes, until you can crush the dal with the back of a wooden spoon. Set aside, covered.

2 Heat the oil in a frying pan and add the mustard seeds. Sizzle for a few seconds until all the seeds have popped.

3 Add the cumin seeds, onion and half the coriander leaves and fry, stirring, until the onion is golden.

4 Add the tomato, turmeric, garlic and chilli, stirring well and mashing the tomato with the spices to make a paste.

5 Add the dal with a little of its cooking water. Stir well, heat through and add salt to taste. Garnish with the remaining coriander leaves.

DAL CURRY II

INGREDIENTS (Serves 4)
350g (12oz) toor dal
50g (2oz) butter or ghee
½ tsp cumin seeds
1½ tbsp gram flour
salt
leaves from 1 sprig of coriander, finely chopped
1-2 green chillies, chopped

1 Pick over the dal and wash it well. Bring about 1.25l (2pt) water to the boil, add the dal and simmer for 10-15 minutes until soft. Strain off excess water and mash the dal well or blend in a liquidizer. Set aside.

2 Heat the butter or ghee in a pan and when hot, fry the cumin seeds for a few seconds until their flavour emerges. Add to the dal.

3 In a small bowl, mix the gram flour with 2-3 tbsp water until it forms a smooth paste.

4 Stir the paste into the dal and simmer on a low heat, stirring occasionally, for about 5 minutes, until it is thick and soupy.

5 Stir in salt to taste and garnish with coriander leaves and green chilli.

(Photograph, see page 30)

DAL AND COCONUT CURRY *(Dal Nariel)*

INGREDIENTS (Serves 2)
175g (6oz) toor dal
1½ tsp turmeric
1½ tsp chilli powder
1 small onion, finely chopped
2-3 tbsp grated coconut
1 tomato, peeled and chopped
2 tbsp oil
4-6 curry leaves
salt

1 Pick over the dal and wash it well. Bring about 850ml(1½pt) water to the boil, add the dal and simmer for 10-15 minutes, until soft and mushy.

2 Stir in the turmeric and chilli powder, cover and keep hot over a low heat.

3 Put half the onion with the coconut in a liquidizer, add 1 tbsp water and blend until smooth. Stir into the dal with the tomato.

4 Heat the oil in a pan and add the mustard seeds. When all the seeds have popped, add the remaining onion and fry until golden. Add to the dal.

5 Stir in the curry leaves and salt to taste.

DAL AND MUSHROOM CURRY *(Kumban Dal)*

INGREDIENTS (Serves 4)
225g (8oz) red split lentils (masoor dal)
1½ tsp turmeric
175-225g (6-8oz) button mushrooms, halved
15g (½oz) fresh ginger, finely grated
1 green chilli, sliced
225g (8oz) onion, chopped
1 tbsp sambar powder
2 tbsp grated or desiccated coconut
225g (8oz) tomatoes, peeled and chopped
2 tbsp oil
1 tsp mustard seeds
4-6 curry leaves
salt

1 Pick over the dal and wash it thoroughly. Cook in about 1.25l (2pt) water with the turmeric, for 10-15 minutes, until it can be crushed under the back of a wooden spoon.

2 Add the mushrooms, ginger, chilli and half of the onion, and cook for a further 10 minutes.

3 Meanwhile, blend the sambar powder with the coconut in a liquidizer, add to the curry with the tomato and cook for a further 6-8 minutes, until the sauce is thick and smooth.

4 Heat the oil in a pan, add the mustard seeds and let them sizzle for a few seconds until they have all popped.

5 Add the curry leaves and remaining onion and fry until the onion is golden. Add to the curry with salt to taste.

(Photograph, see page 31)

ABOVE Dal Curry II
See page 28

ABOVE Dal and Mushroom Curry
(Kumban Dal)
See page 29

CURRIED PUMPKIN AND BLACK-EYED BEANS
(Pethi Lobhia)

INGREDIENTS (Serves 4)
175-225g (6-8oz) black-eyed beans, soaked overnight
225g (8oz) unripe red pumpkin, peeled and thinly sliced
2 green chillies, cut into 4 pieces
2 tbsp coconut oil
4 curry leaves
salt

1 Drain the beans and cook in fresh water for about 10 minutes, until barely tender.

2 Add the pumpkin and green chilli and cook for a further 5-7 minutes, until tender.

3 Mix the coconut oil with 1 tbsp water to release its aroma, then add to the curry with the curry leaves and salt to taste.

(Photograph, see page 34)

SPLIT GRAM AND YAM CURRY
(Koot)

INGREDIENTS (Serves 4)
225g (8oz) split gram (chana dal)
500g (1lb) yams, peeled and cubed
½ tsp turmeric
½ tsp chilli powder
225g (8oz) white pumpkin or green plantain, peeled and cubed
100-175g (4-6oz) grated or desiccated coconut
1 tsp cumin seeds
1 tsp mustard seeds
2-3 tbsp oil
1 red chilli, cut into pieces
6-8 curry leaves
salt

1 Soak the split gram in water with the turmeric and chilli powder for about 2 hours. Drain and cook in about 1.2l (2 pt) water for 15-20 minutes, until the gram can be crushed under the back of a wooden spoon, and most of the water has evaported.

2 Cook the yam and pumpkin or plantain in water to cover for about 15 minutes, until tender but not soft.

3 Add the cooked gram to the vegetables over a low heat, stirring occasionally.

4 Blend three-quarters of the coconut with the cumin seeds in a liquidizer for a few seconds only, and add to the curry.

5 Fry the mustard seeds in the oil until they have all popped, add the red chilli, curry leaves and remaining coconut. Fry for a further 3-4 mintues, stirring, then add to the curry.

6 Take the curry off the heat, cover and leave to stand for 3-4 minutes, then add salt to taste.

(Photograph, see page 35)

CHICKPEAS TORAN
(Chana Toran)

INGREDIENTS (Serves 4)
225g (8oz) chickpeas (garbanzos or whole chana)
4 tbsp oil
1 onion, finely chopped
2 cloves garlic, finely chopped
15g (½ oz) fresh ginger, finely grated
2 green chillies, thinly sliced
leaves from 1 sprig of coriander, finely chopped
salt
½ tsp ground cumin
100g (4oz) tomatoes, sliced
50g (2oz) grated coconut

1 Pick over the chickpeas, wash thoroughly and soak for at least 10 hours in water. Drain and cook in fresh 1ater for 1-1½ hours, depending on the age of the peas, until tender but not soft.

2 Heat the oil in a pan, add the onion and fry until golden.

3 Add the garlic, ginger, green chilli and half the coriander leaves, stir and fry for 3-4 minutes, then drain the chickpeas and stir these in with salt to taste.

4 Heat a small pan without fat or oil, add the ground cumin and cook for 1-2 minutes until the fragrance emerges. Sprinkle over the curry.

5 Garnish with the remaining coriander leaves, the sliced tomatoes and grated coconut.

SPICED CHICKPEAS
(Masala Chana)

INGREDIENTS (Serves 4)
225g (8oz) chickpeas (garbanzos or whole chana)
100g (4oz) butter or ghee
1 onion, finely chopped
2 cloves garlic, finely chopped
15g (½ oz) fresh ginger, finely grated
225g (8oz) tomatoes, peeled and chopped
½ tsp ground coriander
½ tsp chilli powder
1 tbsp mango powder (amchur)
½ tsp ground cumin
1 tsp garam masala
leaves from 1 sprig of coriander
salt

1 Pick over the chickpeas, wash them thoroughly and soak in water for at least 10 hours. Drain and cook in fresh water for 1-1½ hours, depending on the age of the peas, until tender but not soft.

2 Heat the butter or ghee in a pan, add the onion, garlic and ginger and fry until the onion is golden.

3 Add the tomato, ground coriander, chilli, mango powder, cumin, garam masala and half of the coriander leaves. Cook, stirring briskly to mash the tomato with the back of the spoon into a paste.

4 Drain the chickpeas and add, with 2 tbsp of their cooking liquor. Cover and cook on a low heat, stirring occasionally, for about 10 minutes, until the chickpeas have absorbed the flavours of the spices.

5 Sprinkle on the remaining coriander leaves and add salt to taste.

(Photograph, see page 38)

CURRIED CHICKPEAS
(Chana Curry)

INGREDIENTS (Serves 4)
225g (8oz) chickpeas (garbanzos or whole chana)
50-75g (2-3oz) butter or ghee
1 tsp mustard seeds
1 onion, finely chopped
15g (½ oz) fresh ginger, finely grated
1 green chilli, chopped
4-6 curry leaves
50-75g (2-3oz) grated coconut
salt

1 Pick over the chickpeas, wash thoroughly and soak in water for at least 10 hours. Cook in fresh water for 1-1½ hours, depending on the age of the peas, until tender but not soft.

2 Heat the butter or ghee in a pan and add the mustard seeds. Let them sizzle for a few seconds until they have all popped.

3 Add the onion and fry until golden.

4 Drain the chickpeas, reserving the cooking liquor. Add the chickpeas to the pan with the ginger, green chilli and about 2 tbsp cooking liquor. Cover and cook on a low heat, stirring occasionally, for 10 minutes, until the chickpeas have absorbed the flavours of the sauce.

5 Stir in the curry leaves and grated coconut and add salt to taste.

ABOVE Split Gram and Yam Curry
(Koot)
See page 32

OPPOSITE Curried Pumpkin and Black-eyed Beans
(Pethi Lobhia)
See page 32

SPECIAL CURRIED CHICKPEAS
(Chana Curry)

INGREDIENTS (Serves 4)
225g (8oz) chickpeas
½ tsp bicarbonate of soda
100g (4oz) butter or ghee
1 onion
2 or 3 bay leaves
cardamom seeds from 1 pod
2.5cm (1in) cinnamon stick
3 cloves
15g (½ oz) fresh ginger, finely grated
1 tsp fennel seeds
3 cloves garlic, chopped
175g (6oz) tomatoes, peeled and chopped
1 tsp chilli powder
1½ tsp ground cumin
leaves from 1-2 sprigs coriander
½ tsp paprika
2 tsp ground coriander
1 tbsp lemon juice
salt

1. Pick over the chickpeas and wash thoroughly. Soak in water for at least 10 hours. Drain and cook in 1.2l (2 pt) fresh water with the bicarbonate of soda for 1-1½ hours, depending on the age of the peas, until tender but not soft.

2. Heat three-quarters of the butter or ghee in a good-sized pan and add the onion, bay leaves, cardamon seeds, cinnamon, cloves, ginger, fennel seeds, garlic and tomatoes. Fry until the onion is golden, squashing the tomato under the back of a wooden spoon to make a thick paste.

3. Add the chilli powder, half the cumin, the coriander leaves and paprika and cook for 3-4 minutes, stirring occasionally.

4. Add the cooked chickpeas with about 125ml (¼ pt) of their cooking liquor and cook over a low heat for 8-10 minutes.

5. In a separate pan, heat the remaining butter or ghee and when hot, add the remaining ground cumin. Fry for a few seconds, until the fragrance emerges, and add to the chickpeas.

6. Sprinkle on the ground coriander and lemon juice, and add salt to taste.

CHICKPEAS WITH MANGO AND COCONUT
(Aam aur Nariel Ke Chana)

INGREDIENTS (Serves 2)
100g (4oz) chickpeas (garbanzos or whole chana)
flesh of ½ coconut
225g (8oz) green mango, peeled
25g (1oz) butter or ghee
½ tsp ground cumin
salt

1. Pick over the chickpeas, wash thoroughly and soak in water for at least 10 hours. Drain. Cook in fresh water for 1-1½ hours, depending on the age of the peas, until tender but not soft.

2. Chop the coconut flesh and mango into small even pieces and mix with the chickpeas. Heat through in a frying pan for 3-4 minutes, stirring briskly.

3. In a separate pan, heat the butter or ghee and fry the cumin for a few seconds until the fragrance emerges. Add to the vegetables. Add salt to taste.

(Photograph, see page 39)

GREEN LENTIL CURRY
(Moong Curry)

INGREDIENTS (Serves 2)
175g (6oz) whole green lentils (moong dal)
100g (4oz) butter or ghee
1 onion, finely chopped
1 green chilli, chopped
2 cloves garlic, chopped
15g (½ oz) fresh ginger, finely grated
100g (4oz) tomatoes, peeled and chopped
½ tsp turmeric
½ tsp chilli powder
leaves from 1 sprig of coriander
1 tsp cumin seeds
salt

1 Pick over the lentils, wash thoroughly and soak in water for about 4 hours. Drain and cook in fresh water to cover for about 30 minutes, until tender.

2 Meanwhile, heat three-quarters of the butter or ghee in a pan, add the onion, green chilli, garlic and ginger and fry until the onion is golden.

3 Add the tomato and cook, mashing it under the back of a wooden spoon to make a paste.

4 Add the turmeric, chilli powder and coriander leaves and continue to cook until the fat runs clear of the spices.

5 Add the lentils and about 2 tbsp of their cooking liquor and cook for a further 5 minutes.

6 Meanwhile, fry the cumin seeds in the remaining butter or ghee for a few seconds, until the fragrance emerges, then add to the lentils. Add salt to taste.

DRY SPROUTED GREEN LENTIL TORAN
(Moong Dal Toran)

INGREDIENTS (Serves 4)
500g (1lb) sprouted green lentils
2 tbsp oil
¼ tsp asafoetida
1 tsp chilli powder
½ tsp turmeric
1 tsp ground coriander
½ tsp ground cumin
salt
leaves from 1 sprig of coriander
1 tsp lemon juice

1 Heat the oil in a pan, add the asafoetida chilli powder, turmeric, ground coriander and cumin, and fry for a few minutes until the fragrance emerges.

2 Add the sprouted lentils together with 2 tbsp water, ½ tsp salt and half the coriander leaves. Cook, covered, on a low heat, stirring occasionally, for about 10 minutes or until the sprouted lentils are cooked and almost all the water has evaporated.

3 Sprinkle on the lemon juice and the remaining coriander leaves. Add extra salt to taste.

GREEN LENTIL AND BANANA CURRY
(Kela Moong Curry)

INGREDIENTS (Serves 2)
175g (6oz) whole green lentils (moong dal)
1 or 2 hard green bananas, scraped and sliced
½ tsp turmeric
1 green chilli, chopped
salt
100g (4oz) grated or desiccated coconut
½ tsp ground cumin
2 tbsp oil
1 tsp mustard seeds
4-6 curry leaves

1 Pick over the lentils, wash thoroughly and cook in about 850ml (1½ pt) water for about 30 minutes until nearly done.

2 Add the banana, turmeric, chilli and ½ tsp salt, and continue to cook over a low heat.

3 In a liquidizer, blend the coconut with the cumin and 1-2 tbsp water to make a thick paste. Add to the lentils. Stir and cook for 3 minutes to heat through. Add a little water, if necessary, to make a thick sauce.

4 Heat the oil in a frying pan and when hot, add the mustard seeds and the curry leaves. Let them sizzle for a few seconds until all the seeds have popped, then add to the curry. Add extra salt to taste.

ABOVE Spiced Chickpeas
(Masala Chana)
See page 33

OPPOSITE Chickpeas with Mango and Coconut
(Aam aur Nariel Ke Chana)
See page 36

VEGETABLES

Sabzi

India grows a huge variety of vegetables, and combinations of vegetables and spices are endless. Sometimes the spices are used to make a thick sauce, and at other times the vegetables are cooked 'dry' (toran) so that the spices stick to them, making a tasty crunchy 'crust'. Hot spicy vegetables are usually served with rice and mild fragrant ones with bread.

Potatoes and peas are the vegetables most commonly used, with yam (sweet potato) and pumpkin coming next. White pumpkin is not found as commonly as the red variety; instead you can use the dhoody or doddy, a vegetable that has the shape of a small marrow, but the colouring and smoothness of a turnip.

Vegetables like okra and bitter gourd — a distorted cone-shaped pod with a skin as gnarled as a walnut — are now becoming more widely available in England. Drumsticks are still to be had only in Indian grocery shops — these are slim, ridged vegetables up to 30cm (1ft) long, which need to be peeled and cut into suitable lengths before cooking.

Just as vegetables can be used in the making of sweet desserts, fruit can be used in curry: banana and plantain are popular curry ingredients.

BUTTERMILK CURRY
(Morkari)

INGREDIENTS (Serves 4)
600ml (1 pt) soured buttermilk, made by stirring 2 tbsp water into 225g (8oz) yoghurt
225g (8oz) red pumpkin, peeled and cubed
225g (8oz) potatoes, peeled and cubed
1 hard green banana, peeled and thickly sliced
½ tsp turmeric
½ tsp chilli powder
2 tsp salt
grated flesh of ½ coconut
½ tsp ground cumin
2 tbsp oil
1 tsp mustard seeds
½ tsp fenugreek seeds
1 or 2 red chillies, cut into 3 or 4 pieces
6-8 curry leaves

1. Simmer the pumpkin, potato and banana in a pan of water with the turmeric, chilli powder and 1 tsp salt for 10-15 minutes, until cooked. Drain and keep hot.

2. In a bowl, blend the coconut with the cumin, then stir in the buttermilk.

3. Stir the buttermilk mixture into the vegetables over a low heat. Cook for 3-4 minutes, until hot through, stirring all the time, so that the buttermilk does not separate. Set aside, covered.

4. Heat the oil in a frying pan and add the mustard seeds, fenugreek seeds and red chilli. Let them sizzle for a few seconds until all the mustard seeds have popped. Add to the curry.

5. Add salt to taste and sprinkle on the curry leaves.

EXTRA THICK BUTTERMILK CURRY
(Kalan)

INGREDIENTS (Serves 4-6)
600ml (1 pt) soured buttermilk, made by stirring 3 tbsp water into 225g (8oz) yoghurt
225g (8oz) yam, peeled and cubed
1 green plantain, peeled and cubed
225g (8oz) white or red pumpkin, peeled and cubed
½ tsp turmeric
½ tsp chilli powder
grated flesh of 1 small coconut
½ tsp ground cumin
½ tsp ground white pepper
2 green chillies, cut in half
2 tbsp oil
1 tsp mustard seeds
2 red chillies, cut into 3 or 4 pieces
½ tsp fenugreek seeds
8 curry leaves
2 tbsp sugar
2 tsp salt

1. Cook the yam, plantain and pumpkin in water to cover with the turmeric and chilli powder, over a low heat for about 10 minutes, until tender but not soft.

(Photograph, see page 42)

1 Blend the coconut, cumin and pepper and mix well with the buttermilk, then add to the pan with the vegetables and green chillies. Heat through on a low heat for 3-4 minutes, stirring briskly to prevent the buttermilk from separating.

2 Heat the oil in a pan, add the mustard seeds, red chilli, fenugreek seeds and half the curry leaves and let them sizzle for a few seconds, until all the seeds have popped.

3 Stir into the curry with the remaining curry leaves, the sugar and salt to taste.

RIPE MANGO CURRY I
(Aam Curry)

INGREDIENTS (Serves 4-6)
4 small sweet ripe mangoes, peeled and cubed
225g (8oz) yam or potato, peeled and cubed
2 hard green plantains, peeled and cubed
½ tsp turmeric
½ tsp chilli powder
2 green chillies, cut into 4 pieces
grated flesh of ½ coconut
½ tsp cumin seeds
225g (8oz) yoghurt
2 tbsp oil
½ tsp mustard seeds
½ tsp fenugreek seeds
1 red chilli, cut into 4
salt

1 Cook the yam or potato and plantain in water to cover with the turmeric, chilli powder and green chilli for about 6-7 minutes, until half-cooked.

2 Add the mango and continue to cook for a further 6-7 minutes, until the vegetables are tender.

3 Meanwhile, blend the coconut and cumin seeds and stir into the yoghurt.

4 Drain the vegetables, stir in the yoghurt and cook over a low heat, stirring to stop the yoghurt from separating, for 3-4 minutes, until hot through. Cover and set aside.

5 Heat the oil in a frying pan and add the mustard seeds, fenugreek seeds and red chilli. Let them sizzle for a few seconds until all the mustard seeds have popped, then add to the curry. Add salt to taste.

(Photograph, see page 43)

ABOVE Extra Thick Buttermilk Curry
(Kalan)
See page 40

OPPOSITE Ripe Mango Curry I
(Aam Curry)
See page 41

RIPE MANGO CURRY II
(Aam Curry)

INGREDIENTS (Serves 4)
4 small sweet ripe mangoes, cubed, with the skin left on
2 tsp chilli powder
½ tsp turmeric
salt
grated flesh of ½ coconut
½ tsp ground cumin
6 curry leaves
2 tbsp oil
2 tsp mustard seeds
2 tsp fenugreek seeds
2 red chillies, cut into 4 pieces
2-3 tsp sugar

1 Cook the mango in about 600ml (1 pt) water with the chilli powder, turmeric and 1 tsp salt, for about 5 minutes, making sure that the mango does not lose its shape.

2 Blend the coconut with the cumin and add to the mango with half the curry leaves.

3 Heat the oil in a frying pan and when hot, add the mustard seeds. Let them sizzle for a few seconds until they have all popped, then add the fenugreek seeds, red chilli and remaining curry leaves. Stir and fry for a few seconds, then add to the mango. Stir well and add sugar and salt to taste.

MIXED VEGETABLE CURRY
(Aviyal)

INGREDIENTS (Serves 4-6)
1 hard green banana, unpeeled
100g (4oz) runner beans, trimmed
225g (8oz) yam or potato, peeled
100g (4oz) white pumpkin or green papaya, peeled
½ tsp chilli powder
salt
1 tbsp tamarind juice
2 green chillies
3 tbsp grated coconut
6-8 curry leaves
225g (8oz) yoghurt
2 tbsp coconut oil
a little sugar, optional

1 Cook the banana and vegetables in water to cover with the chilli and ½ tsp salt for about 15 minutes, until tender but not soft, stirring occasionally with a wooden spoon. Add the tamarind juice and set aside, covered.

2 Cut the chillies into 4 and crush them with the grated coconut and curry leaves. Stir in the yoghurt and add to the vegetables, mixing well.

3 Mix the coconut oil with a little water to release its fragrance. Pour over the vegetables and add salt to taste. Mix again and add a little sugar, if liked.

(Photograph, see page 46)

VEGETABLE CURRY WITH COCONUT MILK
(Sabzi Nariel)

INGREDIENTS (Serves 4)
flesh of 1 coconut, grated
500g (1lb) ripe white pumpkin, peeled and cubed
1 tbsp coconut oil, mixed with 1 tbsp water
4-6 curry leaves
salt

1 Blend the coconut in a liquidizer with 1 tbsp boiling water. Transfer to a piece of muslin and squeeze out the milk into a bowl. Return the coconut to the liquidizer, add another tbsp boiling water and repeat the process, straining the milk into a separate bowl.

2 Cook the pumpkin in water to cover on a low heat for about 10 minutes, until tender, then add the second bowl of coconut milk and bring to the boil. Remove the pan from the heat.

3 Stir in the first bowl of coconut milk, add the coconut oil, curry leaves and salt to taste.

VEGETABLE CURRY WITH ROASTED COCONUT
(Eliseri)

INGREDIENTS (Serves 2-3)
100g (4oz) toor dal
500g (1lb) red pumpkin, cubed
1 tsp chilli powder
½ tsp turmeric
salt
50-75g (2-3oz) grated or desiccated coconut
1 tsp ground cumin
6-8 curry leaves
3 tbsp oil
1 tsp mustard seeds
2 red chillies, cut into pieces

1 Pick over the dal, wash it thoroughly and cook in about 1.2l (2 pt) water for about 15 minutes, until you can mash it under the back of a wooden spoon.

2 Meanwhile, cook the pumpkin in water for about 12 minutes, until tender.

3 Drain the dal and the pumpkin, reserving a little of the cooking liquor, and mix the two together with the chilli, turmeric and ½ tsp salt. Cook over a low heat, stirring, for 3-4 minutes, adding a little of the cooking liquor if the mixture threatens to stick. Cover and set aside.

4 Blend half the coconut with the cumin and half the curry leaves. Stir into the curry.

5 Heat the oil in a frying pan and when hot, add the mustard seeds and red chilli. Let them sizzle for a few seconds until all the mustard seeds have popped. Add the remaining grated coconut and curry leaves and fry, stirring briskly, for a few seconds until the fragrance of roasted coconut emerges.

6 Fold the fried spice mixture into the curry and add salt to taste.

VEGETABLE CURRY, TAMIL STYLE
(Sambar)

INGREDIENTS (Serves 4-6)
350g (12oz) toor dal
4 drumsticks (see page 40)
1 aubergine
2 medium potatoes
1 medium onion, quartered and sliced
½ tsp turmeric
salt
3-4 tbsp tamarind juice
3 tbsp sambar powder
1 tomato, cut into 8 pieces
1 tbsp oil
1 tsp mustard seeds
4-6 curry leaves
2 tsp sugar
leaves from 1 sprig of coriander

1 Pick over the dal, wash it thoroughly and cook in about 1.2l (2 pt) water for about 15 minutes, until you can mash it under the back of a wooden spoon.

2 Meanwhile, scrape the drumsticks and chop into 5cm (2in) lengths. Peel the aubergine and potatoes and cut into cubes, dropping them in a pan of water as you go to prevent discoloration.

3 Add the aubergine, potato and onion to the cooked dal, with a little extra water if necessary, and cook for about 8 minutes, until the vegetables are half-cooked.

4 Add the drumsticks, turmeric and ½ tsp salt, and continue cooking for about 10 minutes, until the vegetables are tender.

5 Stir in the tamarind juice, sambar powder and tomato, cover and keep hot.

6 Heat the oil in a pan and add the mustard seeds and curry leaves. Let them sizzle for a few seconds, until all the mustard seeds have popped, then add to the curry.

7 Stir in sugar and salt to taste and garnish with coriander leaves.

RIGHT Mixed Vegetable Curry
(Aviyal)
See page 44

VEGETABLE CURRY, KERALA STYLE
(Sambar)

INGREDIENTS (Serves 4-6)
350g (12oz) toor dal
½ tsp turmeric
100-175g (4-6oz) okra, trimmed and cut into 2.5cm (1in) lengths
3 tbsp oil
1 medium onion, quartered and sliced
225g (8oz) potatoes, cubed
2 tomatoes, peeled and chopped
2 tbsp tamarind juice
75-100g (3-4oz) grated coconut
4-6 curry leaves
2 tbsp sambar powder
1 tsp mustard seeds
1 red chilli, cut into 4 pieces
salt
coriander leaves, to garnish

1 Pick over the dal, wash it thoroughly and cook in about 1.2l (2 pt) water with the turmeric for about 15 minutes, until you can mash it under the back of a wooden spoon.

2 Meanwhile, fry the okra in 1 tbsp oil, turning gently, until all the oil is absorbed. This seals the okra and helps it keep its shape. Set aside.

3 When the dal is ready, stir in the onion and potato and continue to cook gently on a low heat for about 8 minutes, until the vegetables are half-cooked.

4 Add the tomato and okra and cook for a further 10 minutes, until the vegetables are tender, adding a little extra water if the pot threatens to boil dry.

5 Stir in the tamarind juice, cover and keep hot.

6 Fry the coconut and half the curry leaves in 1 tbsp oil, then blend with the sambar powder and add to the vegetables.

7 Heat the remaining oil, add the mustard seeds and the red chilli and let them sizzle for a few seconds until all the mustard seeds have popped. Add to the curry.

8 Stir in salt to taste and garnish with coriander leaves.

(Photograph, see page 51)

POTATO CURRY
(Aloo Dum)

INGREDIENTS (Serves 2)
225g (8oz) potatoes, peeled and cubed
15g (½ oz) fresh ginger, finely grated
1 green chilli, chopped
1 onion, finely sliced
½ tsp turmeric
½ tsp chilli powder
50g (2oz) grated coconut
1 tbsp oil
1 tsp mustard seeds
4 curry leaves
salt

1. Cook the potato in water to cover with the ginger, green chilli, onion, turmeric and chilli powder for about 15 minutes, until tender but not soft.

2. Meanwhile, blend the coconut in a liquidizer and add to the cooking potato.

3. Heat the oil in a pan and add the mustard seeds and curry leaves. Let them sizzle for a few seconds until all the seeds have popped, then add to the potato.

4. Leave to stand, tightly covered, for 5-10 minutes, then add salt to taste.

DRY SPICED POTATO
(Aloo Masala)

INGREDIENTS (Serves 4)
500g (1lb) new potatoes
100g (4oz) butter or ghee
1 onion, chopped
15g (½ oz) fresh ginger, finely grated
2 cloves garlic, finely chopped
leaves from 1 sprig of coriander
175g (6oz) tomatoes, peeled and chopped
½ tsp garam masala
½ tsp chilli powder
½ tsp mango powder (amchur)
salt
½ tsp ground cumin

1. Scrub the potatoes and cut into 4. Put them in a pan of cold water to prevent discoloration.

2. Heat three-quarters of the butter or ghee in a pan and add the onion, ginger, garlic and half the coriander leaves. Fry until the onion turns golden.

3. Add the tomato, garam masala, chilli and mango powder, stirring well to mix and squashing the tomato under the back of a wooden spoon to make a paste.

4. Drain the potato and add to the pan with 1-2 tbsp water. Cover and cook on a low heat for about 20 minutes, until the potato is tender but not soft, and all the water has been absorbed. Add salt to taste.

5. Heat the remaining butter or ghee in a separate pan and fry the cumin for 3-4 minutes until the fragrance emerges. Add to the cooked potato and garnish with the remaining coriander leaves.

(Photograph, see page 50)

ABOVE Vegetable Curry, Kerala Style
(Sambar)
See page 48

OPPOSITE Dry Spiced Potato
(Aloo Masala)
See page 49

POTATO MASALA CURRY
(Aloo Masala)

INGREDIENTS (Serves 4)
3 or 4 medium potatoes, cubed
1 large onion, finely chopped
½ tsp turmeric
salt
2 green chillies, chopped
2 tsp garam masala
2 tbsp grated or desiccated coconut
15g (½ oz) fresh ginger, finely grated
2 tbsp oil
1 tsp mustard seeds
4-6 curry leaves
leaves from 1 sprig of coriander

1 Cook the potato in just enough water to cover with three-quarters of the onion, the turmeric, ½ tsp salt and the green chilli, for about 8 minutes, until half-cooked.

2 Meanwhile, blend the garam masala, coconut and ginger in a liquidizer. Add to the potato and continue to cook for a further 8 minutes, until tender but not soft.

3 Heat the oil in a frying pan and add the mustard seeds. Let them sizzle for a few seconds until they have all popped, then add the remaining chopped onion and fry until golden. Stir into the curry.

4 Add salt to taste and sprinkle on the curry and coriander leaves.

(Photograph, see page 54)

POTATO CURRY WITH COCONUT MILK
(Aloo Nariel)

INGREDIENTS (Serves 4)
500g (1lb) potatoes, cubed
flesh of 1 coconut, grated
225g (8oz) onion, chopped
15g (½ oz) fresh ginger, finely grated
2 green chillies, sliced
salt
4-6 curry leaves
2 tbsp coconut oil

1 Blend the coconut in a liquidizer with 1 tbsp boiling water. Transfer to a piece of muslin and squeeze out the milk into a bowl. Return the coconut to the liquidizer, add another tbsp boiling water and repeat the process, straining the milk into a separate bowl.

2 Put the potato and onion in a pan with the second quantity of coconut milk, topping up with water to cover if necessary. Add the ginger, green chilli and 1 tsp salt, and cook for about 15 minutes, until tender but not soft.

3 Add the curry leaves and the coconut oil mixed with 1 tbsp water to release its fragrance. Take off the heat and stir in the remaining coconut milk.

PUMPKIN AND POTATO CURRY
(Aloo Pethi)

INGREDIENTS (Serves 2)
225g (8oz) unripe red pumpkin peeled and cubed
100g (4oz) potato, peeled and cubed
1 tbsp sambar powder
2 tbsp oil
½ tsp mustard seeds
1 small onion, chopped
4-6 curry leaves
¼ tsp asafoetida
½ tsp turmeric
1 red chilli
100g (4oz) tomatoes, peeled and chopped
salt

1 Sprinkle the sambar powder over the potato and pumpkin. Stir well to coat and leave aside.

2 Heat the oil in a pan and add the mustard seeds. Let them sizzle for a few seconds until they have all popped, then add the onion, curry leaves, asafoetida, turmeric and red chilli. Stir well and fry until the onion is golden.

3 Add the marinated vegetables, the tomato and enough water to just cover and simmer for about 15 minutes over a low heat, until the vegetables are tender but not soft and the sauce is thick. Add salt to taste.

RIPE PLANTAIN CURRY WITH YOGHURT
(Kela Dahi)

INGREDIENTS (Serves 4)
2 or 3 ripe plantains, peeled and thickly sliced
½ tsp chilli powder
½ tsp turmeric
4-6 tbsp grated or desiccated coconut
½ tsp cumin seeds or ground cumin
225g (8oz) yoghurt
2 tbsp oil
1 tsp mustard seeds
1 red chilli, cut into 3 or 4 pieces
6-8 curry leaves
2-3 tbsp brown sugar
salt

1 Cook the plantain in about 600ml (1 pt) water with the chilli powder and turmeric for 5 minutes, until tender but not soft, and most of the water has evaporated.

2 Grind or pound the coconut with the cumin (or blend in a liquidizer), then mix with the yoghurt.

3 Stir the yoghurt into the plantain over a low heat. Cook for 3-4 minutes to heat through, stirring all the time to prevent the yoghurt from separating. Cover and set aside.

4 Heat the oil in a pan and when hot, add the mustard seeds. Let them sizzle for a few seconds until they have all popped, then add the red chilli and half the curry leaves. Continue to fry for a few seconds, then add to the curry.

5 Stir in sugar and salt to taste and sprinkle with the remaining curry leaves.

MUSTARD CURRY
(Pachadi)

INGREDIENTS (Serves 4)
4-6 tbsp grated or desiccated coconut
2-3 green chillies, sliced
2 tsp mustard seeds
500g (1lb) unripe red pumpkin or ripe green papaya, cubed
225g (8oz) yoghurt
2 tbsp oil
1 red chilli, chopped
4-6 curry leaves
2 tsp sugar
salt

1 Grind or pound the coconut, green chilli and half the mustard seeds into a fine paste, then mix with the yoghurt.

2 Cook the pumpkin or papaya in just enough water to cover for about 15 minutes until tender, and most of the water has evaported.

3 Stir in the yoghurt over a low heat. Cook for 3-4 minutes to heat through, stirring all the time to prevent the yoghurt from separating.

4 Heat the oil in a pan and fry the remaining mustard seeds. Let them sizzle for a few seconds until they have all popped, then add the red chilli and curry leaves. Continue to fry, stirring, for a few seconds, then add to the curry. Add sugar and salt to taste.

RIGHT Potato Masala Curry
(Aloo Masala)
See page 52

GREEN BEANS AND POTATO TORAN
(Aloo Hari Moong Toran)

INGREDIENTS (Serves 2)
225g (8oz) green beans, trimmed and cut into 2.5cm (1in) lengths
225g (8oz) potatoes, peeled and diced
50-75g (2-3oz) butter or ghee
1 small onion, finely chopped
225g (8oz) tomatoes, peeled and finely chopped
½ tsp garam masala
½ tsp turmeric
½ tsp chilli powder
1 green chilli, cut into pieces
15g (½ oz) fresh ginger, finely grated
1 clove garlic, finely chopped
leaves from 1 sprig of coriander
salt

1 Heat the butter or ghee in a large saucepan and fry the onion until golden.

2 Add the tomato, stir well and squash it with the back of a wooden spoon until it forms a paste.

3 Add the garam masala, turmeric and chilli powder and continue to fry, stirring, for about 5 minutes.

4 Add the beans, potatoes, green chilli, ginger, garlic and coriander leaves with 1 tbsp water and cook gently over a low heat, with the lid tightly on, stirring occasionally, for 10-15 minutes, until the vegetables are done. Add salt to taste.

(Photograph, see page 59)

GREEN BEANS TORAN I
(Hari Moong Toran)

INGREDIENTS (Serves 2)
225g (8oz) green beans, trimmed and cut into 2.5cm (1in) lengths
1 tbsp oil
1 tsp mustard seeds
1 red chilli, cut into 4 or 6 pieces
4-6 curry leaves
1 small onion, finely chopped
salt
50-75g (2-3oz) grated coconut

1 Heat the oil in a heavy bottomed saucepan and when hot, add the mustard seeds. Let them sizzle for a few seconds until they have all popped.

2 Add the red chilli, curry leaves and onion and fry gently, stirring, until the onion is golden.

3 Turn the heat to low and, add the beans, 1 tbsp water, ½ tsp salt and the coconut. Cook, with the lid firmly on, for about 10 minutes, until the beans are tender but not soft, stirring occasionally.

4 Let the pot stand for about 5 minutes and add extra salt if necessary before serving.

GREEN BEANS TORAN II
(Hari Moong Toran)

INGREDIENTS (Serves 2)
225g (8oz) green beans, trimmed and cut into 2.5cm (1in) lengths
1 or 2 green chillies, chopped
75g (3oz) grated coconut
4-6 curry leaves
1 clove garlic, chopped
½ tsp turmeric
2 tbsp oil
2 tsp polished split black lentils (urid dal)
1 tsp mustard seeds
salt

1 Crush the green chilli with the coconut, curry leaves and garlic and mix with the green beans and turmeric in a heavy-bottomed saucepan. Add 1-2 tbsp water and cook over a very low heat, covered tightly, for 10-15 minutes, until tender. Stir occasionally to prevent sticking.

2 Heat the oil in a pan, add the dal and fry until golden.

3 Add the mustard seeds and let them sizzle for a few seconds until they have all popped. Add to the beans and cook for a further 3-4 minutes.

4 Let the pot stand off the heat, covered, for 3-4 minutes, then add salt to taste.

DRY SPICED CABBAGE
(Gobi Bhaji)

INGREDIENTS (Serves 4)
500g (1lb) cabbage
2 tbsp oil
½ tsp ground cumin
½ tsp ground coriander
½ tsp turmeric
¼ tsp asafoetida
½ tsp chilli powder
225g (8oz) potatoes
salt

1 Cut the cabbage into strips, and peel and finely chop the potatoes.

2 Heat the oil and fry the cumin, coriander, turmeric, asafoetida and chilli for 3-4 minutes, until the fragrance of the spices emerges.

3 Add the cabbage and potato, sprinkle on 1-2 tbsp water and ½ tsp salt, cover the pan tightly and cook on a low heat for 5-6 minutes, until the potato is cooked.

4 Take the pot off the heat and let it stand, covered, for 3-4 minutes. Add extra salt to taste.

(Photograph, see page 58)

ABOVE Green Beans and Potato Toran
(Aloo Hari Moong Toran)
See page 56

OPPOSITE Dry Spiced Cabbage
(Gobi Bhaji)
See page 57

CABBAGE TORAN
(Gobi Toran)

INGREDIENTS (Serves 2)
500g (1lb) cabbage, very finely chopped or grated
2 tbsp oil
1-2 tsp polished split black lentils, (urid dal)
½ tsp mustard seeds
4-6 curry leaves
1 small onion, finely chopped
1 green chilli, sliced
15g (½ oz) fresh ginger, finely grated
½ tsp turmeric
50-75g (2-3oz) grated coconut
salt

1 Heat the oil in a large pan, big enough to hold the cabbage. Add the dal and fry until golden.

2 Add the mustard seeds and let them sizzle for a few seconds until they have all popped.

3 Add the curry leaves, onion, green chilli and ginger and continue to fry, stirring, for 3-4 minutes.

4 Stir the cabbage into the pan with the turmeric, cover tightly and cook for about 4 minutes on a low heat until tender but not soft.

5 Stir in the grated coconut and add salt to taste.

MASHED AUBERGINE
(Baigan Bharta)

INGREDIENTS (Serves 2)
1 aubergine
50-75g (2-3oz) butter or ghee
1 onion, finely chopped
leaves from 1 sprig of coriander
1 clove garlic, chopped
15g (½ oz) fresh ginger, finely grated
½ tsp garam masala
1 green chilli, sliced
½ tsp turmeric
½ tsp cumin
½ tsp chilli powder
225g (8oz) tomatoes, peeled and chopped
salt
1 tbsp lemon juice

1 Put the aubergine in a roasting tin and cook in the oven at 200°C/400°F/Gas 6 for 40 minutes or until the inside is cooked. Allow the aubergine to cool, then peel off the skin and immerse the vegetable in cold water.

2 Heat the butter or ghee in a pan and add the onion, half the coriander leaves, the garlic, ginger, garam masala, green chilli, turmeric, cumin and chilli powder. Stir and fry until the onion is golden.

3 Add the tomatoes, squashing well with the back of a wooden spoon to make a paste.

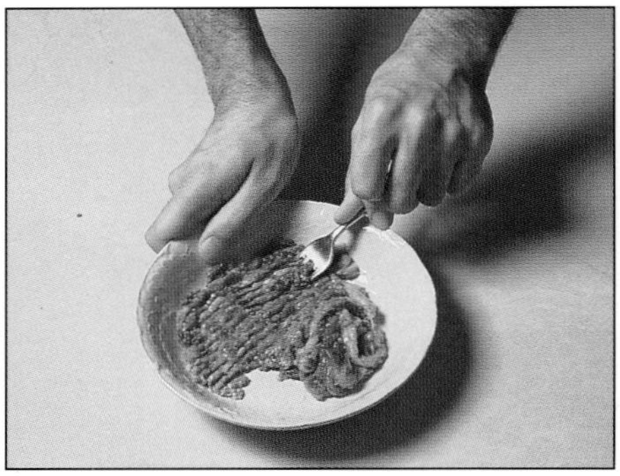

4 Meanwhile, drain the aubergine and mash with a fork.

5 When the butter runs out of the spice paste, add the aubergine and ½ tsp salt, stir thoroughly and cook for 3-4 minutes to heat through.

6 Sprinkle on the remaining coriander leaves and the lemon juice. Add more salt to taste if liked.

(Photograph, see page 62)

AUBERGINE AND POTATO TORAN
(Baigan Aloo Toran)

INGREDIENTS (Serves 4)
300g (10oz) small aubergines
225g (8oz) potatoes
15g (½ oz) fresh ginger, finely grated
2 cloves garlic, chopped
leaves from 1 sprig of coriander
1 tsp ground coriander
½ tsp chilli powder
½ tsp garam masala
½ tsp turmeric
juice from 25-50g (1-2 oz) seedless tamarind
1 small onion, finely chopped
2 tbsp oil
salt

1 Cut the aubergines into large chunks, peel and cube the potatoes and leave the vegetables in a pan of cold water to prevent discoloration while you prepare the spices.

2 In a liquidizer, blend together the ginger, garlic, coriander leaves, powdered spices, tamarind juice and onion.

3 Heat the oil in a pan and add the blended spices. Stir and fry for 3-4 minutes, until the oil runs clear of the spices.

4 Drain the vegetables, add them to the pan and cook, tightly covered, over a low heat for 15-20 minutes, until tender. Add 1-2 tbsp water during the cooking if necessary and stir occasionally to prevent the vegetables from sticking.

5 Add salt to taste.

STUFFED OKRA
(Sabu Bhindi)

INGREDIENTS (Serves 2)
225g (8oz) okra
½ tsp paprika
½ tsp chilli powder
1 tbsp mango powder (amchur)
½ tsp ground ginger
salt
4 tbsp oil

1 Wash the okra and dry on absorbent kitchen paper. Cut off the stalks and slice the okra in half lengthways.

2 Mix together the spices and salt.

3 Stuff the okra with the spice mix and leave them to stand in a cool place for at least 30 minutes.

4 Heat the oil and fry the okra for about 4 minutes, turning carefully, to cook on all sides.

(Photograph, see page 63)

ABOVE Mashed Aubergine
(Baigan Bharta)
See page 60

ABOVE Stuffed Okra
(Sabu Bhindi)
See page 61

OKRA TORAN
(Bhindi Toran)

INGREDIENTS (Serves 2)
300g (10oz) okra
3 tbsp oil
½ tsp mustard seeds
1 tsp polished split black lentils (urid dal)
1 small onion, chopped
15g (½ oz) fresh ginger, finely grated
2 green chillies, chopped
25-50g (1-2 oz) grated or desiccated coconut
4-6 curry leaves
salt

1 Wash the okra and dry on absorbent kitchen paper. Cut into 2cm (¾in) lengths.

2 Fry the okra in 2 tbsp oil, turning frequently, until all the oil has been absorbed. This seals the okra and helps them keep their shape during cooking. Remove the okra from the pan with a slotted spoon and set aside.

3 Add the remaining oil to the pan and when hot, add the mustard seeds and dal. Let them sizzle for a few seconds until all the mustard seeds have popped and the dal is golden, then add the onion and fry until golden.

4 Add the ginger and green chilli and continue to fry for 3-4 minutes, then add the okra and fry for a further 3-4 minutes. Stir in the coconut and curry leaves. Add salt to taste.

OKRA CURRY
(Bhindi Curry)

INGREDIENTS (Serves 2)
225g (8oz) okra
3 tbsp oil
grated flesh of ½ coconut
½ tsp chilli powder
½ tsp turmeric
½ tsp ground cumin
225g (8oz) yoghurt
½ tsp mustard seeds
1 red chilli, cut into pieces
leaves from 1 sprig of coriander, chopped
4-6 curry leaves
salt

1 Wash the okra and dry them on absorbent kitchen paper. Cut into 2.5cm (1in) lengths.

2 Heat 1 tbsp oil and fry the okra for about 2 minutes, turning gently, until all the oil has been absorbed. Removed with a slotted spoon and set aside.

3 Blend the coconut with the chilli powder, turmeric and cumin in a liquidizer, adding 1 tbsp water to make a smooth paste. Mix this into the yoghurt.

4 Heat the remaining oil and when hot, add the mustard seeds and red chilli. Let them sizzle for a few seconds, until all the seeds have popped, then add the okra.

5 Turn the heat down and add the yoghurt mix. Cook gently for 2-3 minutes, stirring to prevent the yoghurt from separating, until hot through. Add the coriander and curry leaves, and salt to taste.

FRIED SPICED OKRA
(Bhindi Masala)

INGREDIENTS (Serves 2)
225g (8oz) okra
50g (2oz) butter or ghee
1 small onion, finely chopped
1 clove garlic, finely chopped
1 green chilli, chopped
15g (½ oz) fresh ginger, finely grated
leaves from 1 sprig of coriander
100g (4oz) tomatoes, peeled and roughly chopped
½ tsp ground corinader
½ tsp turmeric
½ tsp chilli powder
1 tsp garam masala
salt

1 Wash the okra and dry them on absorbent kitchen paper. Cut into 2.5cm (1in) lengths. Heat half the butter or ghee in a pan, add the okra and fry gently. Keep turning them so that they are cooked on all sides, until most of the fat has been absorbed (about 2 minutes). Remove with a slotted spoon and set aside.

2 Add the remaining butter or ghee to the pan and when hot, add the onion, garlic, green chilli, ginger and coriander leaves. Stir and fry until the onion is golden.

3 Add the tomato, ground coriander, turmeric, chilli powder and garam masala and continue to cook, mashing the tomato under the back of a wooden spoon to make a paste.

4 When the butter runs clear of the spices, add the okra and cook on a low heat, stirring occasionally, for about 10 minutes. Add salt to taste.

STUFFED BITTER GOURDS
(Sabu Karela)

INGREDIENTS (Serves 4)
500g (1lb) bitter gourds
1 tsp salt
1 tsp chilli powder
2 tbsp mango powder (amchur)
4 tbsp oil

1 Scrape the gourds and slit them lengthways from the tip, leaving the 2 halves joined at the stalk. Sprinkle salt both inside and out and leave the gourds in a cool place for 15 minutes.

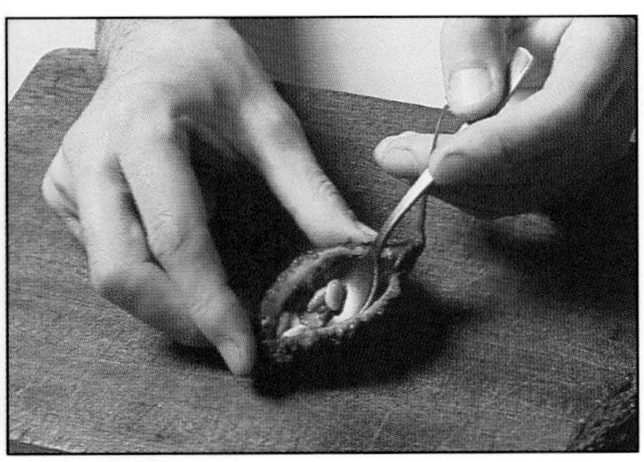

2 Scrape away the seeds and squeeze the gourds to remove the moisture drawn from them by the salt.

3 Mix together the chilli powder, mango powder and remaining salt.

4 Sprinkle the insides of the gourds with oil and stuff the spice mixture well down inside them. Tie the gourds together with thread.

5 Heat the remaining oil over a low heat and fry the gourds, turning gently for 5-10 minutes, until cooked. Remove thread.

6 Serve hot or cold.

(Photograph, see page 67)

BITTER GOURD WITH ONION STUFFING
(Piyaz Karela)

INGREDIENTS (Serves 2)
225g (8oz) bitter gourds
salt
1 onion, finely chopped
1 tsp chilli powder
15g (½ oz) fresh ginger, finely grated
2 tbsp lemon juice
4 tbsp oil

1 Scrape the gourds and slit them lengthways from the tip, leaving the 2 halves joined at the stalk. Sprinkle salt both inside and out and leave the gourds in a cool place for 15 minutes.

2 Scrape away the seeds and squeeze the gourds to remove the moisture drawn from them by the salt.

3 In a liquidizer, blend together the onion, chilli, ½ tsp salt and the ginger, then mix in the lemon juice.

4 Stuff the gourds with the onion mixture and tie them together with thread. Leave to stand for 5-10 minutes.

5 Heat the oil in a pan, add the gourds and fry over a low heat, turning gently, for 5-10 minutes, until done.

RIGHT Stuffed Bitter Gourds
(Sabu Karela)
See page 65

FRIED BITTER GOURD
(Karela Masala)

225g (8oz) bitter gourds
salt
4 tbsp oil
1 green chilli, sliced
15g (½ oz) fresh ginger, finely grated
6-8 curry leaves
2 tbsp lemon juice

1 Scrape the gourds and cut into 2cm (¾in) slices. Sprinkle with 1 tsp salt and leave in a cool place for 10 minutes. Rinse carefully and dry on absorbent kitchen paper.

2 Heat the oil in a pan and add the gourds, green chilli, ginger and curry leaves. Fry for 10-15 minutes, stirring, until the gourd is cooked.

3 Sprinkle over the lemon juice and add salt to taste.

(Photograph, see page 71)

CAULIFLOWER WITH COCONUT MILK
(Nariel Phul Gobi)

INGREDIENTS (Serves 4)
500g (1lb) cauliflower, cut into florets, tough stalks discarded
flesh of 1 coconut, grated
100g (4oz) potatoes, peeled and cubed
15g (½ oz) fresh ginger, finely grated
½ tsp turmeric
½ tsp sambar powder
1 small onion, finely chopped
1 green chilli, sliced
4-6 curry leaves
2-3 tbsp oil
1 tsp mustard seeds
salt
leaves from 1 sprig of coriander

1 Blend the coconut in a liquidizer with 1 tbsp boiling water. Transfer to a sheet of muslin and squeeze the milk into a bowl. Return the coconut to the liquidizer and repeat the process.

2 Simmer the cauliflower and potato in the coconut milk with the ginger, turmeric, sambar powder, three-quarters of the onion and the chilli for about 12 minutes, until the vegetables are tender but not soft. Add the curry leaves.

3 Meanwhile, heat the oil in a pan and when hot, add the mustard seeds. Let them sizzle for a few seconds until they have all popped.

4 Add the remaining onion and fry until golden, then add to the curry.

5 Add salt to taste and garnish with coriander leaves.

CAULIFLOWER WITH COCONUT AND SPICES
(Nariel Phul Gobi Masala)

INGREDIENTS (Serves 4)
500g (1lb) cauliflower
75g (3oz) potato
100g (4oz) grated coconut
1 green chilli
15g (½ oz) fresh ginger, finely grated
1 clove garlic, finely chopped
leaves from 1 sprig of coriander
½ tsp turmeric
1 small onion, finely chopped
4 cashew nuts
2 tbsp oil
1 tsp mustard seeds
4-6 curry leaves
1 red chilli, cut into 4 pieces
75g (3oz) tomatoes, chopped
2 tsp lemon juice
salt

1 Peel the potato and cut into chunks. Divide the cauliflower into florets, discarding the tough stalks. Put the vegetables in a pan of cold water to prevent discoloration.

2 In a liquidizer, coarsely blend the coconut, green chilli, ginger, garlic, coriander leaves, turmeric, onion and cashew nuts.

3 Drain the vegetables, turn them in the spice mixture to coat and leave for about 10 minutes to absorb the flavours.

4 Heat the oil in a pan and when hot, add the mustard seeds, half the curry leaves and the red chilli. Leave them to sizzle for a few seconds until all the seeds have popped.

5 Add the spiced vegetables and tomatoes to the pan, cover and cook on a low heat, stirring occasionally, for about 10 minutes, until the potato is tender but not soft.

6 Sprinkle over the lemon juice, stir in the remaining curry leaves and add salt to taste.

CAULIFLOWER WITH POTATO AND TOMATOES
(Aloo Gobi Tamatar Masala)

INGREDIENTS (Serves 4)
500g (1lb) cauliflower
75g (3oz) potato
50g (2oz) butter or ghee
1 small onion, finely chopped
15g (½ oz) fresh ginger, finely grated
1 clove garlic, finely chopped
2 green chillies, cut into 4-6 pieces
leaves from 1 sprig of coriander
100g (4oz) tomatoes, peeled and roughly chopped
½ tsp chilli powder
½ tsp turmeric
½ tsp ground coriander
½ tsp fennel seeds
½ tsp garam masala
1 tsp ground cumin
salt

1 Peel the potato and cut into chunks. Divide the cauliflower into florets, discarding the tough stalks. Put the vegetables in a pan of cold water to prevent discoloration.

2 Heat three-quarters of the butter or ghee in a heavy-bottomed pan and add the onion, ginger, garlic, green chilli and half the coriander leaves. Stir and fry until the onion is golden.

3 Stir in the tomato, add the chilli powder, turmeric, coriander, fennel seeds, garam masala and half the cumin and cook over a low heat, squashing the tomato under the back of a wooden spoon to make a thick paste.

4 Drain and add the vegetables with about 4 tbsp water. Cover and cook, stirring occasionally, for about 15 minutes, until the potato is tender but not soft.

5 Meanwhile, heat the remaining butter or ghee in a separate pan and when hot, add the remaining ground cumin. Add to the curry with the remaining coriander leaves and salt to taste.

(Photograph, see page 70)

SPICED CAULIFLOWER AND POTATO
(Aloo Gobi Masala)

INGREDIENTS (Serves 4)
500g (1lb) cauliflower
100g (4oz) potato
1 onion, chopped
15g (½ oz) fresh ginger, finely grated
1 tsp ground coriander
½ tsp ground cumin
1 clove garlic, finely chopped
1 tsp fennel seeds
½ tsp turmeric
½ tsp chilli powder
1 tsp garam masala
leaves from 1 sprig of coriander
juice from 25g (1oz) tamarind
2 tbsp oil
salt

1 Peel the potato and cut into chunks. Divide the cauliflower into florets, discarding the tough stalks. Put the vegetables in a pan of cold water to prevent discoloration.

2 In a liquidizer, blend together the onion, ginger, ground coriander, cumin, garlic, fennel seeds, turmeric, chilli powder, garam masala and coriander leaves with the tamarind juice and about 1 tbsp water, to form a thick paste.

3 Heat the oil in a pan and add the spice paste. Fry for a few minutes until the oil runs free from the spices.

4 Drain the vegetables and add to the pan with 1-2 tbsp water. Cover and cook on a low heat, stirring occasionally, for 10-15 minutes, until tender but not soft. Add salt to taste.

ABOVE Cauliflower with Potato and Tomatoes
(Aloo Gobi Tamatar Masala)
See page 69

OPPOSITE Fried Bitter Gourd
(Karela Masala)
See page 68

RED PEPPERS STUFFED WITH VEGETABLES *(Lal Mirchi Sabzi)*

INGREDIENTS (Serves 4)
4 large red peppers
175g (6oz) potatoes
50-75g (2-3oz) butter or ghee
1 small onion, finely chopped
15g (½ oz) fresh ginger, finely grated
1 clove garlic, finely chopped
100g (4oz) tomatoes, peeled and chopped
½ tsp turmeric
½ tsp chilli powder
salt
½ tsp ground coriander
½ tsp garam masala
leaves from 1 sprig of coriander
2 tbsp oil

1 Peel the potatoes, dice them and leave in a pan of cold water to prevent discoloration.

2 Heat the butter or ghee in a pan, add the onion, ginger and garlic and fry until the onion is golden.

3 Add the tomato, turmeric, chilli powder, ½ tsp salt and ground coriander, cook and stir briskly, squashing the tomato under the back of a wooden spoon to make a thick paste.

4 Drain the potato and add to the spice mix with 2-4 tbsp water. Cover and cook on a low heat, stirring occasionally, for 10-15 minutes, until the potato is tender but not soft.

5 Add the garam masala and coriander leaves. Cook for a further 3-4 minutes, then set aside, covered.

6 Wash the peppers and with a sharp knife, cut off the top, which can be used as a lid. Scrape them out and discard the seeds and pith.

7 Stuff the peppers with the potato curry and replace the lids.

8 Heat the oil in a pan, put in the peppers and fry gently on all sides until cooked, about 15 minutes. Alternatively, stand the peppers in a greased dish, cover and cook in the oven at 200°C/400°F/Gas 6 for 30 minutes, until tender.

(Photograph, see page 74)

GREEN PEPPERS STUFFED WITH MEAT
(Mirchi Gosht)

INGREDIENTS (Serves 4)
4 large green peppers
100g (4oz) potato
100g (4oz) butter or ghee
1 small onion, finely chopped
15g (½ oz) fresh ginger, finely grated
2 cloves garlic, finely chopped
100g (4oz) tomatoes, roughly chopped
½ tsp turmeric
1 tsp ground coriander
½ tsp garam masala
½ tsp fennel seeds
leaves from 1 sprig of coriander
½ tsp chilli powder
225g (8oz) lean minced meat (beef or lamb)
1 tsp lemon juice
salt
2tbsp oil

1 Peel the potato, dice and leave in a pan of cold water to prevent discoloration.

2 Heat the butter or ghee in a pan, add the onion, ginger and garlic and fry until the onion is golden.

3 Add the tomato, turmeric, ground coriander, garam masala, fennel seeds, half the coriander leaves and the chilli powder and continue to fry for a few minutes until the fat runs clear of the spices.

4 Drain the potato and stir in into the pan with the minced meat. Cook for 10-15 minutes, stirring occasionally, until cooked through.

5 Sprinkle on the lemon juice, add salt to taste and take off the heat.

6 Wash the peppers and with a sharp knife, cut off the top, which can be used as a lid. Scrape them out and discard the seeds and pith.

7 Stuff the peppers with the curry and replace the lids.

8 Heat the oil in a pan, put in the peppers and fry gently on all sides until cooked, about 15 minutes. Alternatively, stand the peppers in a greased dish, cover and cook in the oven at 200°C/400°F/Gas 6 for 30 minutes, until tender.

CARROT TORAN
(Gajar Toran)

INGREDIENTS (Serves 2)
225g (8oz) carrots, peeled and diced
50g (2oz) toor dal
salt
2 tbsp oil
1 tsp mustard seeds
4 curry leaves
1 or 2 green chillies, seeded and sliced
75g (3oz) grated or desiccated coconut

1 Pick over the dal, wash thoroughly and cook in water to cover for 15 minutes, until it can be crushed under the back of a wooden spoon and almost all the water has been absorbed.

2 Cook the carrots in salted water to cover for 10 minutes, until just tender. Drain and add to the dal.

3 Heat the oil in a pan and when hot, add the mustard seeds, curry leaves and chilli. Let them sizzle for a few seconds until all the seeds have popped, then add to the carrots.

4 Stir in the coconut and heat through over a low flame for 2-3 minutes, stirring, until the curry is quite dry. Add salt to taste.

GREEN PAPAYA TORAN
(Papaya Toran)

INGREDIENTS (Serves 2)
500g (1lb) unripe green papaya, peeled and cubed
salt
2 tbsp oil
2 tsp polished split black lentils (urid dal)
1 small onion, finely chopped
1 tsp mustard seeds
4-6 curry leaves
1 red chilli, cut into 4 or 6 pieces
100g (4oz) grated or desiccated coconut

1 Cook the papaya in salted water to cover for 10-15 minutes, until tender but not soft. Drain and keep hot.

2 Heat the oil in a frying pan and add the dal, onion, mustard seeds, curry leaves and red chilli. Fry until the onion is golden, then add the papaya, stir and fry for 3-4 minutes.

3 Stir in the grated coconut and add salt to taste.

(Photograph, see page 75)

ABOVE Red Peppers Stuffed with Vegetables
(Lal Mirchi Sabzi)
See page 72

ABOVE Green Papaya Toran
(Papaya Toran)
See page 73

BANANA KOFTA
(Kela Kofta)

INGREDIENTS (Serves 4)
4 hard green bananas
1 egg, beaten
15g (½ oz) fresh ginger, finely grated
1 clove garlic, finely chopped
1 green chilli, chopped
leaves from 1 sprig of coriander
100g (4oz) butter or ghee
1 small onion, finely chopped
½ tsp tomato purée
½ tsp garam masala
1 tomato, peeled and chopped
½ tsp chilli powder
½ tsp turmeric
1 tbsp ground cashew nuts
225g (8oz) yoghurt
4 curry leaves
salt

1 Scrape off the tough skin of the bananas (but do not peel) and slice thickly. Cook them in about 600ml (1 pt) water for about 20 minutes, until soft.

2 Drain and mash the banana, and mix with the egg.

3 Blend or pound the ginger, garlic, green chilli and half the coriander leaves, using a liquidizer or pestle and mortar. Add to the mashed banana and mix well.

4 Form the banana mixture into small balls and set aside. Heat the butter or ghee in a pan, add the onion and remaining coriander leaves and fry until the onion is golden.

5 Add the tomato purée, garam masala and tomato and cook, squashing the tomato under the back of a wooden spoon to make a thick paste.

6 Add the chilli powder, turmeric and ground cashews, then stir in the yoghurt. Add 1-2 tbsp water to thin down the sauce if liked and, when it is bubbling, add the banana balls. Simmer for 3-4 minutes, then add the curry leaves and salt to taste.

BANANA TORAN
(Kela Toran)

INGREDIENTS (Serves 2)
2 hard green bananas
salt
3 tbsp oil
½ tsp mustard seeds
1 small onion, finely chopped
4-6 curry leaves
¼ tsp asafoetida
½ tsp ground coriander
½ tsp chilli powder
100g (4oz) tomatoes, peeled and chopped

1 Scrape the bananas and cut in 2 lengthways, then slice them and sprinkle with 1 tsp salt. Leave for 2 or 3 minutes, then rinse and dry on absorbent kitchen paper.

2 Heat the oil, add the mustard seeds and fry until they pop.

3 Add the onion and curry leaves and fry until the onion is golden.

4 Add the asafoetida, coriander, chilli powder and tomato and cook for a further 4-5 minutes, stirring occasionally.

5 Add the banana and cook for a further 15 minutes, until tender. Add salt to taste.

SPINACH TORAN
(Palak Toran)

INGREDIENTS (Serves 2)
500g (1lb) fresh spinach
4 tbsp oil
1 small onion, finely chopped
1 green chilli, chopped
75g (3oz) tomatoes, peeled and chopped
75g (3oz) grated or desiccated coconut
salt

1 Wash the spinach, discard any discoloured leaves and tough stalks, and shake dry. Chop as finely as possible and leave in a colander to drain.

2 Heat the oil in a pan and gently fry the onion and green chilli until the onion is transparent.

3 Add the spinach and tomato, cover tightly and cook on a low heat for 4-5 minutes, shaking the pan occasionally, until the spinach has collapsed.

4 Stir in the coconut and add salt to taste.

(Photograph, see page 78)

VEGETABLE BIRIYANI
(Sabzi Biriyani)

INGREDIENTS (Serves 4-6)

FOR THE VEGETABLES
225g (8oz) tomatoes, peeled and chopped
100g (4oz) carrots, peeled and diced
225g (8oz) potatoes, peeled and diced
100g (4oz) fresh peas
½ tsp fennel seeds
½ tsp turmeric
cardamom seeds from 1 pod
2.5cm (1in) cinnamon stick
3 cloves
1 tsp poppy seeds
2 cloves garlic, chopped
15g (½ oz) fresh ginger, grated
2 green chillies, chopped
leaves from 1 sprig of coriander
50g (2oz) butter or ghee
1 small onion, chopped
2 bay leaves
salt

FOR THE RICE
300-350g (10-12oz) basmati rice
50g (2oz) butter or ghee
1 onion, finely chopped
1 bay leaf
about 50g (2oz) cashew nuts
50g (2oz) ghee

1 Grind or pound the fennel seeds, turmeric, cardamom seds, cinnamon, cloves and poppy seeds. Blend in a liquidizer with the garlic, ginger, green chilli and coriander leaves.

2 Heat the butter or ghee in a pan, add half the onion and fry until golden.

3 Add the blended spices, the bay leaves and tomato and continue to cook, mashing the tomato under the back of a wooden spoon to make a thick paste.

4 Pour on 300ml (½pt) water, add the carrots, potatoes, peas and ½ tsp salt and bring to the boil. Simmer for about 15 minutes, until the potatoes are cooked, and the sauce is thick.

5 Meanwhile, prepare the rice. Pick over the rice, wash in 2 or 3 changes of water, then soak for 15-20 minutes. Drain thoroughly.

6 Heat the butter or ghee in a pan, add the onion and crumble over the bay leaf. Fry until the onion is golden.

7 Pour on enough boiling water to cover the rice and cook, covered, for 10 minutes. Then turn off the heat and leave, covered, for 5-10 minutes until the liquid is absorbed and the rice is tender but not soft.

8 Stir the vegetables into the rice and heat through. Add extra salt to taste.

9 Fry the cashew nuts briefly in ghee and sprinkle over the curry.

(Photograph, see page 79)

ABOVE Vegetable Biriyani
(Sabzi Biriyani)
See page 77
OPPOSITE Spinach Toran
(Palak Toran)
See page 76

MEAT DISHES

Gosht

Goat is the meat most often eaten in India, and lamb is the best substitute. Shoulder or neck are the best cuts to buy as they have more connective tissue. This means that they can be cooked for a fairly long time and end up succulent and tender.

All recipes in this section are intended for boned meat, but the bones can be left in. If you wish to do this, allow for the weight of the bones, which will be about half the total weight of the meat.

Beef and pork may also be used, although beef is not often eaten in India. For the Hindus, the cow is a sacred animal, and the Muslims are forbidden pork.

The meat you choose should be lean. Trim it carefully of any fat, gristle etc. It is a mistake to think that you can make a good curry with leftover pieces of meat. Curries involve long, slow simmering to extract the juices from the meat, so meat that has had all its juices extracted for some other purpose will not be much good.

Young tender meat is the best to choose for kebabs, as these require faster cooking.

MEAT CURRY IN A THICK SAUCE *(Gosht Dupiaza)*

INGREDIENTS (Serves 4)
1kg (2lb 3oz) meat, trimmed and cubed
1 small onion, finely chopped
2 tbsp oil
1 tbsp plain flour
1 tbsp lemon juice
½ tsp ground pepper
salt
50g (2oz) butter or ghee
225g (8oz) tomatoes, chopped
1 green chilli, sliced
leaves from 1 sprig of coriander
½ tsp garam masala

1 Fry the onion in the oil until golden. Add the flour and continue to fry, stirring, until the flour is coloured and has formed a paste.

2 Add the meat, lemon juice, pepper and ½ tsp salt, stir and pour on about 850ml (1½ pt) water. Bring to the boil and simmer, covered, for about 1 hour, stirring occasionally, until the meat is tender and the sauce is thick.

3 Heat the butter or ghee in a pan, add the tomato and green chilli and fry gently, stirring, for 3-4 minutes, then add to the meat.

4 Sprinkle on the coriander leaves and garam masala.

(Photograph, see page 83)

MEAT CURRY WITH YOGHURT
(Dahi Gosht)

INGREDIENTS (Serves 4)
1kg (2lb 3oz) meat, trimmed and cubed
4-6 tbsp oil
2 onions, roughly chopped
25g (1oz) fresh ginger, chopped
2 cloves garlic, chopped
1 green chilli, chopped
cardamom seeds from 2 pods
2.5cm (1in) cinnamon stick
3 cloves
½ tsp fennel seeds
1 tbsp ground coriander
1 tsp ground cumin
leaves from 2 sprigs coriander
½ tsp turmeric
1 tsp chilli powder
125g (5oz) yoghurt
4-6 curry leaves
salt

1 Heat half the oil in a pan, add half the onion, the ginger, garlic, green chilli, cardamom seeds, cinnamon, cloves, fennel seeds, ground coriander, cumin, half the coriander leaves, the turmeric and chilli and fry gently, stirring, for 10 minutes.

2 Take the pan off the heat and stir in the yoghurt. Mix well and set aside.

3 Chop the remaining onion finely and fry in the remaining oil until golden. Add the meat and fry for about 15 minutes, stirring occasionally.

4 Stir in the spiced yoghurt and cook gently for 8-10 minutes, stirring.

5 Pour on about 600ml (1 pt) boiling water, turn down the heat and cook, covered, for about 1 hour or until the meat is tender. Cook uncovered if a thicker sauce is required and stir frequently.

6 Sprinkle on the curry leaves and remaining coriander leaves and add salt to taste.

(Photograph, see page 82)

PLAIN MEAT CURRY
(Gosht Curry)

INGREDIENTS (Serves 4)
1kg (2lb 3oz) meat trimmed and cubed
1 tbsp lemon juice
salt
2 tbsp ground coriander
2 tsp chilli powder
½ tsp ground pepper
1 tsp ground cumin
½ tsp turmeric
50g (2oz) butter or ghee
1 tbsp oil
1 small onion, finely chopped
25g (1oz) fresh ginger, chopped
2 cloves garlic, chopped
1 tsp garam masala
4-6 curry leaves

1 Wash the meat thoroughly in hot water. Drain and cook, covered, in 600ml (1 pt) fresh water with the lemon juice and a pinch of salt for about an hour or until the meat is tender and most of the liquid has evaporated.

2 Meanwhile, mix the coriander, chilli, pepper, cumin and turmeric with 2 tbsp water to make a smooth paste.

3 Heat the butter or ghee in a pan with the oil, add the onion, ginger and garlic and fry until the onion is golden.

4 Add the spice paste and continue to fry for 10 minutes. Add the paste to the cooked meat with ½ tsp salt and cook, covered, on a low heat for 10-15 minutes, until the sauce is thick.

5 Sprinkle on the garam masala and the curry leaves and add extra salt to taste.

ABOVE Meat Curry with Yoghurt
(Dahi Gosht)
See page 81

ABOVE OPPOSITE Meat Curry in a Thick Sauce
(Gosht Dupiaza)
See page 80

BELOW OPPOSITE Meat and Tomato Curry
(Tamatar Gosht)
See page 84

MEAT AND TOMATO CURRY
(Tamatar Gosht)

INGREDIENTS (Serves 4)
1kg (2lb 3oz) meat, trimmed and cubed
50g (2oz) butter or ghee
1 small onion, finely chopped
15g (½ oz) fresh ginger, finely grated
3 cloves garlic, finely chopped
225g (8oz) tomatoes, peeled and chopped
½ tsp turmeric
2 tsp chilli powder
1 tbsp ground coriander
½ tsp ground cumin
salt
1 tsp garam masala
225g (8oz) potatoes, peeled and diced
leaves from 1 sprig of coriander

1 Heat the butter or ghee in a large saucepan, add the onion, ginger and garlic and fry until the onion is golden.

2 Add the tomato, turmeric, chilli powder, ground coriander, cumin, ½ tsp salt and garam masala. Stir and continue to fry until the fat runs clear of the spices, then add 600ml (1 pt) boiling water and mix well.

3 Add the meat and cook, covered, over a low heat for about 1 hour, until tender and the sauce is thick.

4 Add the potato and a little extra water, if necessary, and cook for a further 10-15 minutes until tender but not soft.

5 Sprinkle on the coriander leaves and extra salt to taste.

(Photograph, see page 83)

SWEET AND SOUR MEAT CURRY
(Chuteraney)

INGREDIENTS (Serves 4)
1kg (2lb 3oz) meat, trimmed and cubed
2 tbsp oil
50g (2oz) butter or ghee
2 onions, finely chopped
1 green chilli, chopped
15g (½ oz) fresh ginger, finely grated
2 cloves garlic, crushed
225g (8oz) tomatoes, peeled and chopped
leaves from 2 sprigs of coriander
½ tsp garam masala
½ tsp turmeric
1 tsp chilli powder
225g (8oz) potatoes, peeled and chopped
½ tsp ground pepper
1 tbsp sugar
125g (5oz) yoghurt
2 tbsp lemon juice

1 Heat the oil and butter or ghee in a pan, add the onion, green chilli, ginger and garlic and fry until the onion turns golden.

2 Add the tomato, half the coriander leaves, the garam masala, turmeric and chilli powder and cook, stirring and squashing the tomato under the back of a wooden spoon until it makes a paste and the fat has run clear of the spices.

3 Add the meat and 600ml (1 pt) boiling water and cook over a low heat for about 1 hour, until tender.

4 Add the potato and cook for a further 10-15 minutes until tender but not soft.

5 Mix the remaining coriander leaves, the pepper and sugar with the yoghurt, add to the curry and cook for 2-3 minutes, stirring, to heat through.

6 Sprinkle on the lemon juice and add salt to taste.

(Photograph, see page 86)

MEAT CURRY WITH ROASTED SPICES
(Masala Gosht)

INGREDIENTS (Serves 4)
500g (1lb) meat, trimmed and cubed
3 tbsp oil
2 tbsp coriander seeds
2 red chillies, cut into pieces
2.5cm (1in) cinnamon stick
3 cloves
50g (2oz) grated coconut
½ tsp turmeric
salt
2 green chillies, sliced
15g (½ oz) fresh ginger, grated
1 small onion, chopped
225g (8oz) potatoes, peeled and diced
225g (8oz) tomatoes, peeled and chopped
6 curry leaves

1 Heat half the oil in a pan and fry the coriander seeds, red chilli, cinnamon, cloves and coconut for about 5 minutes, then transfer to a grinder or a mortar and reduce to a smooth paste.

2 Put the meat in a bowl with the turmeric, ½ tsp salt, green chilli, ginger and half the onion, add the spice paste and mix well. Leave to marinate for 15 minutes.

3 Heat the remaining oil in a large saucepan and fry the remaining onion until golden.

4 Add the marinated meat, the potato and tomato, pour on 850ml (1½ pt) boiling water, cover and cook on a low heat for about 1 hour, until the meat is tender and the sauce is thick.

5 Add extra salt to taste and sprinkle on the curry leaves.

(Photograph, see page 87)

FRIED SPICED MEAT KEEMA
(Keema Masala)

INGREDIENTS (Serves 4)
500g (1lb) lean minced meat
100g (4oz) butter or ghee
1 onion, finely chopped
2 cloves garlic, finely chopped
15g (½ oz) fresh ginger, finely grated
leaves from 1 sprig of coriander
175g (6oz) tomatoes, peeled and chopped
cardamom seeds from 2 pods, crushed
2.5cm (1in) cinnamon stick
3 cloves
1 bay leaf
½ tsp ground coriander
½ tsp turmeric
½ tsp ground cumin
½ tsp chilli powder
salt
225g (8oz) potatoes, peeled and diced

1 Heat the butter or ghee in a pan, add the onion and fry until golden.

2 Add the garlic, ginger, half the coriander leaves, the tomato, cardamom, cinnamon, cloves and bay leaf and fry for 3-4 minutes, stirring.

3 Add the coriander, turmeric, cumin, chilli powder and ½ tsp salt and stir to make a thick paste.

4 Add the meat and potato and fry for about 15 minutes, stirring occasionally, then pour on 300ml (½pt) boiling water, cover and cook on a low heat for a further 15 minutes, until the meat and potato are cooked and the sauce is thick.

5 Add salt to taste and sprinkle on the remaining coriander leaves.

(Photograph, see page 86)

ABOVE Sweet and Sour Meat Curry
(Chuteraney)
See page 84

ABOVE Fried Spiced Meat Keema
(Keema Masala)
See page 85

ABOVE Meat Curry with Roasted Spices *(Masala Gosht)*

See page 85

SPICED MEAT BIRIYANI
(Biriyani Gosht)

INGREDIENTS (Serves 4)
1kg (2lb 3oz) meat, trimmed and cubed
50g (2oz) grated coconut
50g (2oz) whole cashew nuts
1 tbsp chopped mint leaves
leaves from 2 sprigs coriander
25g (1oz) fresh ginger, thinly sliced
4 cloves garlic, thinly sliced
1 green chilli, sliced
1 small onion, thinly sliced
125g (5oz) yoghurt
1 tbsp lemon juice
2 tsp biriyani masala
1 tsp ground coriander
salt
300g (10oz) basmati rice, washed and soaked in water for 2 hours
2 tbsp ghee
2 tbsp milk
cashew nuts, almonds and sultanas to decorate

1 In a liquidizer, blend the coconut, cashews, mint and coriander leaves to make a smooth paste.

2 Stir in the ginger, garlic, green chilli, onion, yoghurt, lemon juice, biriyani masala, ground coriander and ½ tsp salt.

3 Turn the meat in this mixture to coat and leave to marinate for about 5 minutes.

4 Put the meat in a heavy-bottomed pan, pour on 600ml (1 pt) boiling water, cover and cook over a low heat for about an hour, until tender.

5 Meanwhile, drain the rice and cook in 850ml (1½ pt) boiling water for 10 minutes, until half-cooked. Drain.

6 In a large oven proof casserole, heat the ghee, then add the meat and rice and mix thoroughly. Cook, covered with foil or a lid, in the oven at 150°C/300°F/Gas 2 for 10 minutes.

7 Sprinkle on the milk and decorate with cashews, almonds and sultanas.

MEAT CURRY WITH NUTS AND COCONUT MILK
(Nariel Gosht)

INGREDIENTS (Serves 4)
1kg (2lb 3oz) meat, trimmed and cubed
flesh of 1 coconut, grated
50g (2oz) cashew nuts
2 cloves garlic, chopped
½ tsp chilli powder
15g (½ oz) fresh ginger, grated
½ tsp ground coriander
½ tsp turmeric
leaves from 1 sprig of coriander
½ tsp garam masala
½ tsp ground pepper
100g (4oz) butter or ghee
1 small onion, chopped
¼ tsp saffron
25g (1oz) sultanas
50g (2oz) almonds
salt
4-6 curry leaves

1 Blend the coconut in a liquidizer with 1 tbsp boiling water. Transfer to a sheet of muslin and squeeze out the milk into a bowl. Return the coconut to the liquidizer and repeat the process.

2 Grind, pound or blend in a liquidizer the cashew nuts, garlic, chilli powder, ginger, ground coriander, turmeric, coriander leaves, garam masala and pepper.

3 Heat the butter or ghee in a pan, add the onion and fry until golden, then add the blended spices and fry for a further 5 minutes.

4 Add the meat, stir and fry for 5 minutes, then pour on the coconut milk, add the saffron, sultanas, almonds and ½ tsp salt and cook, covered, over a low heat for about 1 hour, until the meat is tender and the sauce has thickened.

5 Sprinkle on the curry leaves.

(Photograph, see page 90)

MEATBALL AND CAULIFLOWER CURRY
(Phul Gobi Kofta)

INGREDIENTS (Serves 4)

FOR THE MEAT AND CAULIFLOWER
500g (1lb) lean minced meat
1 egg, beaten
15g (½ oz) fresh ginger, grated
2 cloves garlic, chopped
½ tsp garam masala
½ tsp ground cumin
leaves from 1 sprig of coriander
salt
1 small cauliflower, cut into florets, tough stalks discarded

FOR THE SAUCE
75g (3oz) butter or ghee
1 small onion, finely chopped
cardamom seeds from 2 pods, crushed
2 cloves
2.5cm (1in) cinnamon stick
15g (½ oz) fresh ginger, grated
2 cloves garlic, crushed
½ tsp turmeric
1 tsp chilli powder
½ tsp ground cumin
½ tsp ground coriander
225g (8oz) tomatoes, peeled and chopped or 2 tsp tomato purée
125g (5oz) yoghurt
salt
leaves from 1 sprig of coriander

1 Mix the egg with the minced meat.

2 Grind, pound or blend in a liquidizer the ginger, garlic, garam masala, cumin, coriander leaves and ½ tsp salt.

3 Mix the spice paste with the meat, form it into small balls and set aside.

4 For the sauce, heat the butter or ghee in a pan, add the onion and fry until golden.

5 Add the cardamom seeds, cloves, cinnamon, ginger, garlic, turmeric, chilli powder, cumin and coriander and fry for 3 or 4 minutes, stirring.

6 Add the tomato or tomato puree and cook, stirring, until the fat runs clear of the spices.

7 Stir in the yoghurt with a pinch of salt and 1-2 tbsp water and bring gently to the boil.

8 Carefully slide in the meat balls and cauliflower florets and cook for about 20 minutes on a low heat, stirring occasionally and taking care not to break the meat balls.

9 Sprinkle on the coriander leaves and add salt to taste.

(Photograph, see page 91)

ABOVE Meat Curry with Nuts and Coconut Milk
(Nariel Gosht)
See page 88

OPPOSITE Meatball and Cauliflower Curry
(Phul Gobi Kofta)
See page 89

MEAT KEBABS
(Seekh Kebabs)

INGREDIENTS (Serves 4)
500g (1lb) lean minced meat
15g (½ oz) fresh ginger, finely grated
1 green chilli, chopped
salt
½ tsp garam masala
1 onion, finely chopped
½ tsp chilli powder
½ tsp ground pepper
½ tsp ground cumin
leaves from 1 sprig of coriander
1 egg, beaten
6 tbsp oil

1 Grind, pound or blend in a liquidizer the ginger, green chilli, ½ tsp salt and the garam masala with 1-2 tbsp water to make a paste.

2 In a bowl, mix the spice paste with the meat and onion, sprinkle on the chilli powder, pepper, cumin and coriander leaves, add the egg and 1-2 tsp oil and combine well.

3 Roll the mixture into small sausages and thread on skewers.

4 Grill the kebabs for 20 minutes, basting with a little oil, and turning frequently until cooked through.

5 Remove the kebabs from the skewers and fry in the remaining oil for about 10 minutes, turning gently.

(Photograph, see page 94)

MEAT AND VEGETABLE CURRY
(Sabzi Gosht)

INGREDIENTS (Serves 4)
500g (1lb) meat, trimmed and cubed
75g (3oz) butter or ghee
1 small onion, finely chopped
15g (½ oz) fresh ginger, grated
2 cloves garlic, chopped
½ tsp turmeric
½ tsp chilli powder
½ tsp ground coriander
½ tsp garam masala
½ tsp ground cumin
1 green chilli, chopped
4-6 curry leaves
175g (6oz) tomatoes, peeled and chopped
100g (4oz) okra, trimmed and cut into 2 or 3 pieces
100g (4oz) carrots, peeled and diced
225g (8oz) potatoes, peeled and cubed
175g (6oz) aubergine, peeled and cubed
50g (2oz) fresh peas
salt

1 Heat the butter or ghee in a pan, add the onion and fry until golden.

2 Add the ginger, garlic, turmeric, chilli powder, coriander, garam masala, cumin, green chilli and curry leaves, stir and fry for a further 5 minutes.

3 Add the meat and fry for 5 minutes, then add the tomato, okra, carrot, potato, aubergine and peas, pour on 850ml (1½ pt) water, add ½ tsp salt and cook over a low heat for 1 hour, until the vegetables and meat are tender and the sauce is thick.

4 Add extra salt to taste.

(Photograph, see page 95)

PORK VINDALOO
(Soor Vindaloo)

INGREDIENTS (Serves 4)
1-1.4kg (2lb 3oz-3lb) shoulder of pork, trimmed and cubed
6 cloves garlic
25g (1oz) fresh ginger
4 red chillies, seeded
1 tsp mustard seeds
½ tsp fenugreek seeds
½ tsp turmeric
½ tsp ground cumin
4 tbsp white wine vinegar
2-3 tbsp oil
2 onions, finely chopped
225g (8oz) tomatoes, peeled and chopped
salt
4-6 curry leaves
6 cloves
2.5cm (1in) cinnamon stick
1 tsp sugar

1 Chop 4 cloves garlic with half the ginger, then grind, pound or blend in a liquidizer with the chillies, mustard seeds, fenugreek seeds, turmeric and half the vinegar.

2 Heat the oil, add the onion and fry until golden.

3 Add the spice paste, stir and fry gently for 15 minutes.

4 Add the tomato and continue to cook, mashing it under the back of a wooden spoon to make a paste.

5 When the oil has run clear of the spices, add the pork and fry for 5 minutes, turning the pieces in the spice mixture.

6 Add ½ tsp salt and pour on 600ml (1 pt) boiling water. Simmer, covered, for 40 minutes, until the pork is tender.

7 Slice the remaining garlic and ginger and add with the curry leaves, cloves and cinnamon stick. Cook for a further 5 minutes.

8 Add the sugar and remaining vinegar. Add salt to taste.

(Photograph, see page 95)

OPPOSITE Meat Kebabs
(Seekh Kebabs)
See page 92

RIGHT Meat and Vegetable Curry
(Sabzi Gosht)
See page 92

BELOW Pork Vindaloo
(Soor Vindaloo)
See page 93

CHICKEN DISHES

Murghi

In India chicken used to be a special treat and many spectacular and elegant dishes were devised to make the most of it. Today, however, it makes quite a regular appearance at the tables of meat-eating families.

Older birds have more flavour and these can be used in dishes requiring long slow cooking, which will tenderize the flesh. Quicker cooking dishes call for young birds that are tender in the first place.

Overcooking chicken ruins it — it gets dehydrated, tough and stringy, unlike red meat — and so testing is important. Stick a skewer in the thickest part of the meat, or at a joint, and if the juices run clear and the flesh is white, the meat is done. Chicken should be basted frequently to keep it from drying out and to seal in its natural juices.

You can use chicken joints for most of the recipes in this sections, or buy a whole bird and cut it up into smaller pieces yourself. Indians mostly skin chicken before cooking it to allow the aromatics to permeate the meat.

CHICKEN BIRIYANI

(Murghi Biriyani)

INGREDIENTS (Serves 4-6)

FOR THE CHICKEN
1.4kg (3lb) chicken
1 tbsp biriyani masala
1 green chilli
15g (½ oz) fresh ginger, finely grated
2 cloves garlic, chopped
leaves from 2 sprigs coriander
1 tbsp chopped mint leaves
50g (2oz) cashew nuts
6 tbsp oil
50g (2oz) butter or ghee
1 small onion, chopped
225g (8oz) tomatoes, peeled and chopped
salt

FOR THE RICE
100g (4oz) butter or ghee
2 bay leaves
1 small onion, chopped
225g (8oz) basmati rice, washed, soaked in water for 20 minutes and drained
10 cashew nuts
50g (2oz) sultanas

1 Pound, grind or blend in a liquidizer the biriyani masala, green chilli, ginger, garlic, coriander leaves, mint and cashews, adding about 2 tbsp water to make a paste.

2 Skin the chicken and cut into 8 pieces. Wash in hot water and dry on absorbent kitchen paper.

3 Heat 4 tbsp oil in a pan, add the chicken and fry for about 10 minutes, turning once. Remove the chicken with a slotted spoon and set aside.

4 Add the remaining oil and the butter or ghee to the pan and when hot, add the onion and fry until golden.

5 Add the spice mixture and cook, stirring, until the fat runs clear of the spices.

6 Add the tomato, mashing it with the back of a wooden spoon to make a paste.

7 Add the chicken pieces and salt and pour on 600ml (1 pt) boiling water. Cook for about 1 hour, until the chicken is tender and the sauce has thickened.

8 Meanwhile, for the rice, heat three-quarters of the butter or ghee in a heavy-bottomed saucepan, add the bay leaves and onion and fry until the onion is golden.

9 Pour on the rice and stir well over a low heat for about 10 minutes, until the rice is translucent.

10 Add 600ml (1 pt) boiling water, bring back to the boil and cook on a low heat, covered, for 8-10 minutes. Drain off the water.

11 Mix the rice, chicken and sauce together in an overproof casserole, cover with a lid or foil and cook in the oven at 150°C/300°F/Gas 2 for 10-15 minutes, until the rice is completely cooked. This dish should be moist but not too wet.

12 Fry the cashews and sultanas briefly in the remaining butter or ghee and sprinkle on top of the curry.

(Photograph, see page 99)

CHICKEN WITH HONEY
(Murghi Madh)

INGREDIENTS (Serves 4)
8 chicken legs
15g (½ oz) fresh ginger, finely grated
2 cloves garlic, crushed
2 tbsp lemon juice
4 tbsp runny honey
1 tbsp paprika
1 tsp chilli powder
1 tbsp cornflour
½ tsp salt
50g (2oz) butter or ghee
1 tbsp lemon juice
leaves from 1-2 sprigs coriander

1 Put the ginger and the next 7 ingredients in a mortar or a liquidizer and pound or blend well to make a smooth paste.

2 Wash the chicken pieces, dry them on absorbent kitchen paper and prick them all over with a sharp, pointed knife.

3 Rub the spice paste all over the chicken and leave for at least 20 minutes to marinate.

4 Lay the chicken pieces on a rack across a roasting tin and cook in the oven at 200°C/400°F/Gas 6 for 45 minutes until the meat is cooked through.

5 Sprinkle over the lemon juice and garnish with coriander leaves.

(Photograph, see page 98)

ABOVE Chicken with Honey
(Murghi Madh)
See page 97

OPPOSITE Chicken Biriyani
(Murghi Biriyani)
See page 96

CHICKEN WITH SPICES
(Murghi Masala)

INGREDIENTS (Serves 4)
8 chicken legs
2-3 tbsp oil
2 cloves garlic, chopped
15g (½ oz) fresh ginger, finely grated
leaves from 1 sprig of coriander
½ tsp garam masala
1 tsp ground coriander
1 tsp ground cumin
4 cashew nuts
1 tbsp paprika
1 tsp chilli powder
1 tbsp lemon juice
1-2 tsp salt
125g (5oz) yoghurt

1 In a liquidizer, blend all the ingredients except the chicken and yoghurt to a thick paste, then stir in the yoghurt and mix thoroughly.

2 Wash the chicken pieces, dry on absorbent kitchen paper and prick all over with a sharp pointed knife.

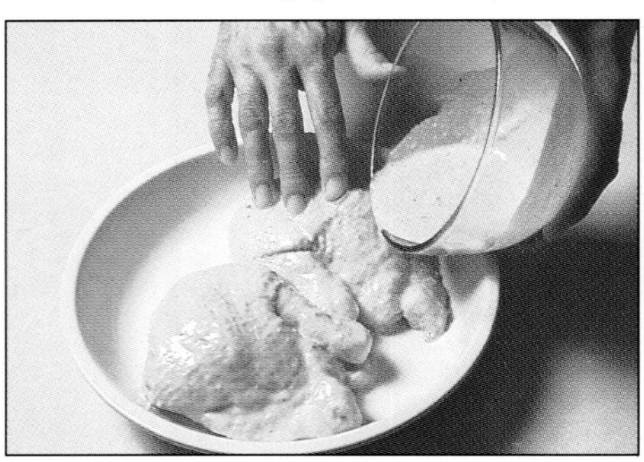

3 Smother the chicken in the spice paste and marinate for about 3 hours.

4 Lay the chicken pieces on a rack across a roasting tin and cook in the oven at 200°C/400°F/Gas 6 for 45 minutes until the chicken is tender.

5 Sprinkle on extra salt to taste.

(Photograph, see page 102)

CHICKEN, TANDOORI STYLE
(Murghi Tandoori)

INGREDIENTS (Serves 4)
8 chicken legs
1-2 tbsp lemon juice
salt
15g (½ oz) fresh ginger, finely grated
3 cloves garlic, chopped
1 tsp ground coriander
½ tsp ground cumin
1 tsp chilli powder
2 tbsp paprika
red food colouring (optional)
1 tsp garam masala
½ tsp ground black pepper
125g (5oz) yoghurt
1 lemon, sliced
1 small onion, sliced

1 Skin the chicken legs, wash thoroughly and dry on absorbent kitchen paper. Slash them with a sharp pointed knife.

2 Rub in the lemon juice and sprinkle with salt.

3 Blend the ginger and garlic in a liquidizer with 1 tbsp water, then mix with the coriander, cumin, chilli powder, paprika, red food colouring, garam masala and pepper and stir into the yoghurt.

4 Smother the chicken legs in the spiced yoghurt and leave, covered, in the fridge to marinate overnight.

5 Lay the chicken legs on a rack across a roasting tin and cook in the oven at 200°C/400°F/Gas 6 for about 45 minutes, until tender.

6 Sprinkle with extra salt to taste and garnish with lemon and onion slices.

(Photograph, see page 103)

CHICKEN AND TOMATO CURRY
(Tamatar aur Murghi)

INGREDIENTS (Serves 4)
1 chicken, about 1.4kg (3lb), skinned and jointed
125g (5oz) butter or ghee
2 onions, chopped
3 cloves garlic, crushed
15g (½ oz) fresh ginger, finely grated
1 green chilli, chopped
cardamom seeds from 2 pods, crushed
3 cloves
2.5cm (1in) cinnamon stick
1 bay leaf
225g (8oz) tomatoes, peeled and chopped
½ tsp turmeric
½ tsp chilli powder
½ tsp paprika
1 tbsp ground coriander
½ tsp fennel seeds
225g (8oz) potatoes, peeled and diced
¼ tsp ground pepper
¼ tsp saffron
salt
leaves from 2 sprigs of coriander

1 Heat the butter or ghee in a pan, add the onion, garlic, ginger, green chilli, cardamom seeds, cloves, cinnamon, and bay leaf and fry until the onion is golden.

2 Add the tomato, and continue to cook, squashing it under the back of a wooden spoon to make a paste.

3 Add the turmeric, chilli powder, paprika, ground coriander and fennel seeds and fry until the fat runs clear of the spices.

4 Add the chicken pieces and fry for 5 minutes, then pour on 850ml (1½ pt) boiling water, add the potato and cook over a low heat, covered, for 1 hour, until the chicken and potato are done and the sauce has thickened.

5 Sprinkle on the pepper, saffron, salt and coriander leaves.

(Photograph, see page 102)

PLAIN CHICKEN CURRY
(Sada Murghi)

INGREDIENTS (Serves 4)
1.4kg (3lb) chicken, skinned and jointed
½ tsp turmeric
½ tsp chilli powder
2 tsp ground coriander
3 tbsp oil
1 onion, finely chopped
½ tsp ground pepper
3 cloves garlic, crushed
15g (½ oz) fresh ginger, finely grated
225g (8oz) tomatoes, peeled and chopped
50g (2oz) butter or ghee
¼ tsp saffron
2-3 tsp sugar
salt
leaves from 1 sprig of coriander

1 Mix the turmeric, chilli powder and ground coriander with 2 tbsp water.

2 Heat the oil in a pan, add the onion and fry until golden.

3 Add the pepper, garlic and ginger, fry for 3-4 minutes until the fragrance emerges, then add the tomato and the spice paste and continue to fry until the oil runs clear of the spices.

4 Add the butter or ghee and when melted, add the chicken pieces and 850ml (1½ pt) boiling water and cook over a low heat for about 1 hour, until the chicken is tender.

5 Sprinkle on the saffron, sugar, salt to taste and coriander leaves.

ABOVE Chicken with Spices
(Murghi Masala)
See page 100

LEFT Chicken and Tomato Curry
(Tamatar aur Murghi)
See page 101

ABOVE Chicken, Tandoori Style
(Murghi Tandoori)
See page 100

CHICKEN CURRY WITH YOGHURT
(Murghi Dahi)

INGREDIENTS (Serves 4)
1.4kg (3lb) chicken, skinned and jointed
4 tbsp oil
2 onions, finely chopped
2 cloves garlic, finely chopped
15g (½ oz) fresh ginger, finely grated
cardamom seeds from 2 pods
2.5cm (1in) cinnamon stick
2 cloves
½ tsp fennel seeds
1 tsp paprika
2 tsp ground coriander
½ tsp ground cumin
½ tsp chilli powder
½ tsp turmeric
125g (5oz) yoghurt
225g (8oz) potatoes, peeled and diced
225g (8oz) tomatoes, peeled and chopped
salt
leaves from 2 sprigs of coriander

1 Heat 3 tbsp oil in a pan, add the onion, garlic, ginger, cardamom seeds, cinnamon, cloves and fennel seeds and fry until the onion is golden.

2 Add the paprika, ground coriander, cumin, chilli powder and turmeric and continue to fry until the oil runs free from the spice mixture.

3 Drain off the oil, stir in the yoghurt and blend in a liquidizer until smooth.

4 Fry the remaining onion in the remaining oil until golden, add the chicken and continue to fry for 5 minutes.

5 Add the blended spice mixture, the potato, tomato, ½ tsp salt and 850ml (1½ pt) boiling water and cook on a low heat for about 1 hour, until the meat and vegetables are done.

6 Add extra salt to taste and sprinkle over the coriander leaves.

(Photograph, see page 107)

CHICKEN KEBABS
(Murghi Kebabs)

INGREDIENTS (Serves 2)
500g (1lb) boned chicken, skinned and cubed
2 tbsp soy sauce
2 tbsp oil
1 tsp ground black pepper

1 Mix the soy sauce, oil and pepper with 1 tbsp water, pour over the chicken, turn to coat and leave to marinate for at least an hour.

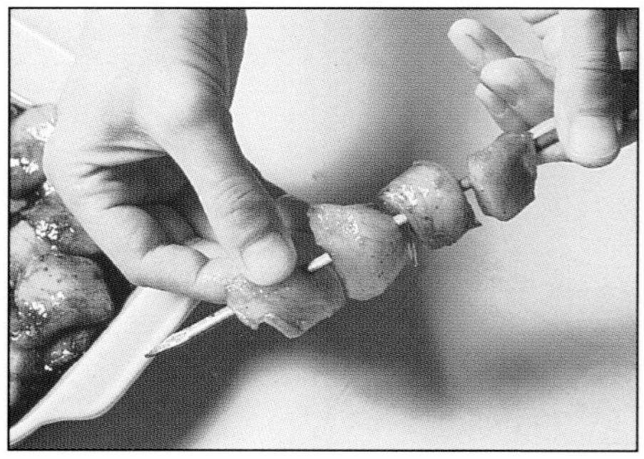

2 Thread the chicken cubes onto skewers and grill slowly for 25-30 minutes, turning and basting occasionally with the marinade, until cooked through.

(Photograph, see page 106)

WHOLE ROAST CHICKEN
(Murghi Masala)

INGREDIENTS (Serves 4)
1 chicken, about 1.4kg (3lb), skinned
½ tsp ground black pepper
salt
50g (2oz) ground almonds
25g (1oz) fresh ginger, finely grated
2 cloves garlic, chopped
leaves from 2 sprigs of coriander
1 onion, finely chopped
1 tsp garam masala
1 tsp paprika
1 tsp chilli powder
1 tsp ground coriander
¼ tsp saffron
1 tsp ground cumin
125g (5oz) yoghurt
1 tbsp lemon juice

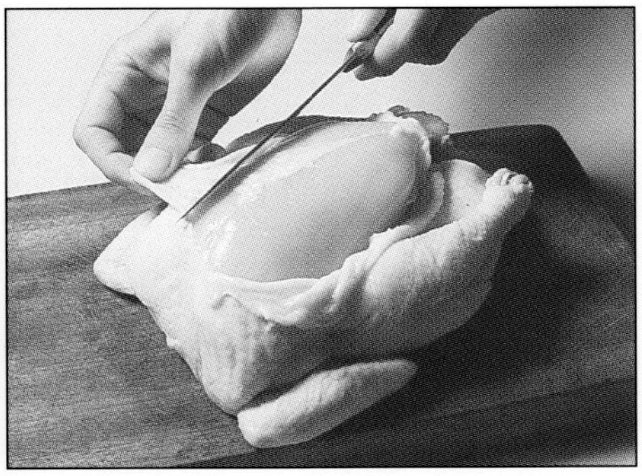

1. Skin and wash the chicken and dry with absorbent kitchen paper. Prick all over with a sharp pointed knife, rub in the black pepper and ½ tsp salt and leave to absorb the flavours for about 30 minutes.

2. Pound, grind or blend in a liquidizer the almond, ginger, garlic, coriander leaves, onion, garam masala, paprika, chilli powder, ground coriander, saffron and cumin, then mix well with the yoghurt.

3. Smother the chicken in the spiced yoghurt and marinate for at least 4 hours.

4. Put the chicken in a roasting tin and cook in the oven at 200°C/400°F/Gas 6, basting occasionally, for up to 2 hours until tender and the juices run clear when the bird is pierced with a skewer.

5. Sprinkle with lemon juice and salt to taste.

(Photograph, see page 107)

SPICED CHICKEN
(Murghi Masala)

INGREDIENTS (Serves 4)
1kg (2lb 3oz) chicken joints, skinned
3 tbsp coriander seeds
2 red chillies, cut into 3 or 4 pieces
2.5cm (1in) cinnamon stick
2 cloves
50g (2oz) grated coconut
½ tsp turmeric
2 onions, finely chopped
15g (½ oz) fresh ginger, finely grated
4-6 curry leaves
3 tbsp oil
2 green chillies, seeded and cut into 3 or 4 pieces
2 bay leaves
100g (4oz) tomatoes, peeled and chopped
salt

1. Heat a pan without any fat or oil until very hot, then add the coriander seeds, red chilli, cinnamon stick and cloves, and roast them for 5-6 minutes, shaking the pan to prevent them from burning. Grind or pound the roasted spices into a fine powder.

2. Blend the spices and coconut together in a liquidizer.

3. Stir in the turmeric, three-quarters of the onion, the ginger and half the curry leaves.

4. Smother the chicken with the spice mixture and leave to marinate for 10-15 minutes.

5. Heat the oil in a pan, add the remaining onion, green chilli and bay leaves. Fry until the onion is golden.

6. Add about 850ml (1½ pt) water to the tomato and chicken pieces and cook gently, covered, for an hour, until the chicken is tender and the sauce is thick.

7. Add salt to taste.

OPPOSITE Chicken Kebabs
(Murghi Kebabs)
See page 104

ABOVE Chicken Curry with Yoghurt
(Murghi Dahi)
See page 104

RIGHT Whole Roast Chicken
(Murghi Masala)
See page 105

FISH & PRAWNS
Machi aur Jhinga

There are said to be over 2,000 varieties of fish and shellfish available in India, and it forms an important part of the diet, especially for non-meat eaters. The cold-water fish that swim in the seas around Europe and America are not natives to the warm waters of the Indian Ocean, but they are equally suited to Indian cooking. Best varieties are the firm-fleshed white fish such as cod, haddock or halibut.

In India, fish are poached, steamed, baked or fried. Fish in batter is very popular: the batter absorbs flavours from the oil as well as keeping the natural flavours of the fish sealed in. Indians enjoy fish barbecued over fragrant wood or wrapped in banana leaves and cooked in the embers of the fire.

When buying fish, always make sure it is very fresh. It should never smell 'fishy'. Use frozen prawns in these recipes if you are unable to get fresh ones.

FISH CURRY
(Machi Kalia)

INGREDIENTS (Serves 2)
500g (1lb) white fish, boned and skinned
4 tbsp oil
1 onion, finely chopped
½ tsp fennel seeds
50g (2oz) grated coconut
1 tsp chilli powder
¼ tsp turmeric
3 tbsp tamarind juice
15g (½ oz) fresh ginger, finely grated
50g (2oz) tomatoes, peeled and chopped
1 green chilli, chopped
salt
4-6 curry leaves

1 Cut the fish into squares about 5cm (2in) and wash well.

2 Heat 3 tbsp oil in a pan add three-quarters of the onion, the fennel seeds and coconut and fry until the onion is golden.

3 Add the chilli powder and turmeric and continue to cook for 4-5 minutes, then pound, grind or blend in a liquidizer.

4 Heat the tamarind juice in a small pan over a low heat and mix in the blended spices, the ginger, tomato and green chilli.

5 Heat until the mixture bubbles then add the fish and ½ tsp salt and cook gently for 10 minutes, until the fish is tender.

6 Meanwhile, fry the remaining onion in the remaining oil until golden. Add to the curry when the fish is cooked.

7 Sprinkle on the curry leaves and add extra salt to taste.

(Photograph, see page 110)

FISH MOLIE
(Mouli)

INGREDIENTS (Serves 2)
500g (1lb) white fish, boned and skinned
salt
flesh of 1 coconut, grated
3 tbsp oil
1 onion, finely chopped
15g (½ oz) fresh ginger, finely grated
2 green chillies, chopped
¼ tsp turmeric
2 tsp ground coriander
1 tsp cornflour
2 tbsp white wine vinegar
4-6 curry leaves

1 Rub the fish with salt, leave for 5 minutes and then rinse under cold running water. Cut into large chunks and set aside.

2 Blend the coconut in a liquidizer with 1-2 tbsp boiling water. Transfer to a sheet of muslin and squeeze the milk into a bowl. Return the coconut to the liquidizer and repeat the process.

3 Heat the oil in a pan, add the onion, ginger, green chilli, turmeric and coriander and fry until the onion is golden.

4 Mix the cornflour with the coconut milk, add to the pan and bring to the boil.

5 Add the fish and ½ tsp salt and cook gently for 10 minutes, until the fish is tender.

6 Add the vinegar, cook for a further minute, then take the curry from the heat and sprinkle on the curry leaves.

(Photograph, see page 111)

CHILLI FRIED PRAWNS
(Jhinga Lal Mirchi)

INGREDIENTS (Serves 2)
225g (8oz) peeled prawns
½ tsp turmeric
1 tsp chilli powder
salt
2 tbsp oil
1 lemon, sliced, for garnish

1 Wash the prawns well and dry them on absorbent kitchen paper.

2 Mix them with the turmeric, chilli powder and ½ tsp salt and leave to marinate for 10 minutes.

3 Heat the oil, add the prawns and fry gently for 5 minutes.

4 Transfer the prawns to a serving dish and decorate with lemon slices.

(Photograph, see page 111)

ABOVE Fish Curry
(Machi Kalia)
See page 108

OPPOSITE ABOVE Fish Molie
(Mouli)
See page 109

OPPOSITE BELOW Chilli Fried Prawns
(Jhinga Lal Mirchi)
See page 109

SARDINES IN A THICK SPICY SAUCE *(Machli Curry)*

INGREDIENTS (Serves 4)
500g (1lb) fresh sardines, cleaned
3 tbsp oil
2 tbsp coriander seeds
3 red chillies, cut into pieces
50-75g (2-3oz) grated coconut
1-2 tbsp tamarind juice
1 green chilli, chopped
15g (½ oz) fresh ginger, finely grated
1 onion, finely chopped
¼ tsp turmeric
salt
4-6 curry leaves

1 Heat half the oil in a pan, add the coriander seeds and red chilli and fry for 3-4 minutes until the fragrance emerges, then grind, pound or blend with the coconut.

2 Return to the pan and continue to fry, adding the tamarind, green chilli, ginger, half the onion and the turmeric, for a further 5-7 minutes, until they make a thick paste.

3 Lay the sardines on a plate, smother them in the paste and leave to marinate for 15 minutes.

4 Meanwhile, heat the remaining oil and fry the remaining onion until golden.

5 Add the marinated sardines to the pan with 2 tbsp water, cover and cook on a low heat for 5-8 minutes, until tender.

6 Add salt to taste and sprinkle on the curry leaves.

(Photograph, see page 115)

PRAWN BIRIYANI *(Jhinga Biriyani)*

INGREDIENTS (Serves 4)

FOR THE PRAWNS
500g (1lb) shelled prawns
1 green chilli
15g (½ oz) fresh ginger, grated
1 clove garlic, chopped
50g (2oz) grated or desiccated coconut
4 cashew nuts
2 tsp biriyani masala
50g (2oz) butter or ghee
1 small onion, chopped
salt
1 tbsp lemon juice
cashew nuts and sultanas, fried in a little butter or ghee, for decoration

FOR THE RICE
50g (2oz) butter or ghee
1 small onion, chopped
2 bay leaves
225g (8oz) basmati rice, washed, soaked in water for 20 minutes and drained
salt
100g (4oz) fresh peas

1 Grind, pound or blend in a liquidizer the chilli, ginger, garlic, coconut, cashews and biriyani masala to make a thick paste.

2 Heat the butter or ghee in a pan, add the onion and fry until golden.

3 Add the blended spice paste and fry for a further 5-8 minutes, stirring.

4 Add the prawns and ½ tsp salt and cook on a low heat for 3-4 minutes, stirring, until the prawns are hot through and coated in the spice mixture.

5 For the rice, heat the butter or ghee in a pan, add the onion and bay leaves and fry until the onion turns golden.

6 Pour on the rice, stir and fry for about 10 minutes, until translucent.

7 Add ½ tsp salt, the peas and enough water to cover and simmer on a low heat for 10-15 minutes, until the rice is almost cooked.

8 Stir the prawns and rice together in an ovenproof casserole, cover with a lid or foil and cook in the oven at 150°C/300°F/Gas 2 for 10-15 minutes.

9 Sprinkle over the lemon juice, cashews and sultanas and add extra salt to taste.

(Photograph, see page 114)

FISH CURRY WITH YOGHURT *(Dahi Machi)*

INGREDIENTS (Serves 2)
500g (1lb) white fish, boned, skinned and cubed
3 tbsp oil
6 cloves garlic, finely chopped
½ tsp fenugreek seeds
1 onion, finely chopped
2 tsp chilli powder
1 tsp ground coriander
salt
225g (8oz) tomatoes, peeled and chopped
125g (5oz) yoghurt
4-6 curry leaves

1 Heat the oil in a pan, add the garlic and fry until golden.

2 Add the fenugreek seeds and continue to cook until lightly browned. Remove garlic and fenugreek with a slotted spoon and keep aside.

3 Add the onion to the pan and fry until golden, then return the garlic and fenugreek to the pan and cook for a further 3-4 minutes.

4 Add the chilli powder and coriander and cook for 3-4 minutes until their fragrance emerges.

5 Pour on about 300ml (½pt) water and bring to the boil. Add ½ tsp salt, then add the fish and tomato and cook gently for 10-15 minutes, until the fish is tender and the sauce is thick.

6 Stir in the yoghurt and curry leaves, taking care not to break up the fish. Heat through for 2-3 minutes and then add extra salt to taste.

(Photograph, see page 114)

ABOVE Fish Curry with Yoghurt
(Dahi Machi)
See page 113

ABOVE Prawn Biriyani
(Jhinga Biriyani)
See page 112

ABOVE Sardines in a Thick Spicy Sauce *(Machli Curry)*
See page 112

FRIED SPICED FISH
(Machi Masala)

INGREDIENTS (Serves 2)
500g (1lb) white fish, boned, skinned and cubed
1 onion, finely chopped
15g (1/2 oz) fresh ginger, finely grated
6 curry leaves
salt
1/4 tsp turmeric
1 tsp chilli powder
4 tbsp oil

1. Pound, grind or blend in a liquidizer the onion, ginger, curry leaves, 1/2 tsp salt, the turmeric and chilli powder to make a thick paste.

2. Spread the paste over the fish and leave to marinate for about 2 hours.

3. Heat the oil in a large pan that the fish will fit in one layer, add the fish and fry for about 10 minutes, until tender.

4. Add extra salt to taste.

(Photograph, see page 118)

BAKED FISH STUFFED WITH MUSHROOMS
(Kumban Machi)

INGREDIENTS (Serves 4)
500-850g (1-1 1/2lb) whole fish, such as cod, cleaned
1 onion, sliced and separated into rings
15g (1/2 oz) fresh ginger, finely grated
1 tsp chopped mint leaves, fresh or bottled
225g (8oz) tomatoes, peeled and chopped
1/2 tsp chilli powder
salt
225g (8oz) mushrooms, peeled and sliced
2 tbsp lemon juice

1. Heat 2 tbsp oil in a pan, add the onion, ginger and mint and fry until the onion is golden.

2. Add the tomato, chilli powder and 1/2 tsp salt and cook, mashing the tomato into a thick paste with the back of a wooden spoon.

3. Add the mushroom and continue to cook for 6-7 minutes.

4. Use this mixture to stuff the fish. Lay it in a greased ovenproof dish, sprinkle with the remaining oil and the lemon juice, cover with foil and bake in the oven at 175°C/350°F/Gas 4 for 30-35 minutes, until tender.

5. Remove skin and serve.

(Photograph, see page 118)

FRIED SPICED PRAWNS

(*Jhinga Masala*)

INGREDIENTS (Serves 2)
225g (8oz) peeled prawns
2 tsp ground coriander
1 tsp chilli powder
½ tsp turmeric
50-75g (2-3oz) grated coconut
100g (4oz) tomatoes, peeled and chopped
1 onion, finely chopped
15g (½ oz) fresh ginger, finely grated
salt
4 tbsp oil
4-6 curry leaves
1 tbsp lemon juice
leaves from 1 sprig of coriander

1 Grind, pound or blend in a liquidizer the ground coriander, chilli powder, turmeric and coconut.

2 Mix with the tomato, half the onion, the ginger and ½ tsp salt. Coat the prawns in this mixture and leave to marinate for 10-15 minutes.

3 Heat the oil, add the remaining onion and the curry leaves and fry until the onion is golden.

4 Add the prawns and cook gently for 10 minutes.

5 Take the curry from the heat, add extra salt to taste and sprinkle over the lemon juice and coriander leaves.

(Photograph, see page 119)

PRAWN VINDALOO

(*Jhinga Vindaloo*)

INGREDIENTS (Serves 4)
500g (1lb) shelled prawns (or langoustines)
½ tsp cumin seeds
25g (1oz) fresh ginger, finely grated
1-2 cloves garlic, finely chopped
1 tsp mustard seeds
3 tbsp oil
2 onions, finely chopped
6 curry leaves
100g (4oz) tomatoes, peeled and chopped
2 tsp chilli powder
½ tsp turmeric
3 tbsp white wine vinegar
1 tsp cornflour, optional
salt
½ tsp sugar, optional

1 Crush the cumin seeds with the ginger, garlic and mustard seeds.

2 Heat the oil in a pan, add the onion and curry leaves and fry until the onion is golden.

3 Add the tomato, chilli powder, turmeric and 1-2 tbsp water and cook, mashing the tomato under the back of a wooden spoon to make a thick paste.

4 Add the crushed spices and continue to fry for 5 minutes, then add the prawns and 4 tbsp water and simmer for 10 minutes.

5 Pour on the vinegar. The sauce may be thickened, if necessary, by mixing the cornflour with 1 tsp water. Add salt to taste and sugar, if liked.

(Photograph, see page 119)

ABOVE Baked Fish with Mushrooms
(Kumban Machi)
See page 116

LEFT Fried Spiced Fish
(Machi Masala)
See page 116

ABOVE OPPOSITE Fried Spiced Prawns
(Jhinga Masala)
See page 117

BELOW OPPOSITE Prawn Vindaloo
(Jhinga Vindaloo)
See page 117

EGGS

Unday

Eggs can be used to make a very quick and satisfying curry. Hard-boiled eggs can be shelled and pierced with the point of a sharp knife to let in the flavours of the sauce they are being cooked in. Curried scrambled eggs make a very speedy lunch for one, as well as an unusual side dish at dinner.

YELLOW RICE WITH HARD-BOILED EGGS *(Unday Ki Biriyani)*

INGREDIENTS (Serves 4-6)
300-350g (10-12oz) basmati rice
100g (4oz) butter or ghee
1 small onion, chopped
2 cloves garlic, chopped
1 green chilli, chopped
cardamom seeds from 2 pods
2 bay leaves
3 cloves
salt
½ tsp turmeric
1 chicken stock cube, optional
10-15 cashew nuts
50g (2oz) ghee
25g (1oz) sultanas
4-6 hard-boiled eggs
1 tsp lemon juice

1 Wash the rice thoroughly in 2 or 3 changes of water, then soak for 10-15 minutes.

2 Heat the butter or ghee in a pan, add the onion, garlic, green chilli, cardamom seeds, bay leaves and cloves, and fry until the onion is golden.

3 Drain the rice, pour it into the pan, stir and fry for 10 minutes, until it turns translucent.

4 Pour on 600ml (1 pt) boiling water, add ½ tsp salt, the turmeric and the stock cube, and simmer over a low heat for 10 minutes. Turn off heat and leave, covered, for 5 minutes until all the moisture has been absorbed and the grains of rice are separate and tender.

(Photograph, see page 122)

5 Fry the cashew nuts for a couple of minutes in the ghee, adding the sultanas for the last few seconds.

6 Cut the eggs in half, sprinkle with lemon juice and rub with salt.

7 Spread the rice in a serving dish, sprinkle with salt to taste and arrange the eggs, cashew nuts and sultanas on top.

CURRIED EGGS
(Unday Ki)

INGREDIENTS (Serves 4-6)
6 hard-boiled eggs
3-4 tbsp oil
2 small onions, grated
15g (½ oz) fresh ginger, grated
2 cloves garlic, crushed
2.5cm (1in) cinnamon stick
1 bay leaf
½ tsp chilli powder
2 tbsp ground coriander
2 cashew nuts, ground
225g (8oz) tomatoes, peeled and chopped
salt
½ tsp garam masala
leaves from 1 sprig of coriander
1 tsp lemon juice
4 peppercorns, crushed

1 Heat the oil in a pan, add the onion, ginger, garlic, cinnamon and bay leaf and fry until the onion is golden.

2 Add the chilli powder, ground coriander, cashew and tomato and continue to cook, mashing the tomato under the back of a wooden spoon to make a thick paste.

3 Pour on 125ml (¼ pt) water with ½ tsp salt, bring to the boil and add the eggs. Cook over a low heat for 5 minutes.

4 Take the curry off the heat and sprinkle on the garam masala, coriander leaves, lemon juice and pepper. Add extra salt to taste.

(Photograph, see page 123)

ABOVE Yellow Rice with Hard-Boiled Eggs
(Unday Ki Biriyani)
See page 120

ABOVE Curried Eggs
(Unday Ki)
See page 121

WHOLE EGGS FRIED WITH SPICE
(Unday Masala)

INGREDIENTS (Serves 4-6)
6 hard-boiled eggs
2 tbsp oil
2 tsp ground coriander
1 tsp chilli powder
¼ tsp ground pepper
salt
2 tbsp lemon juice

1 Make several cuts into the eggs with the point of a sharp knife to allow the spices to enter.

2 Heat the oil, add the coriander, chilli powder, pepper and salt and fry for about 3 minutes.

3 Add the lemon juice and stir to make a paste.

4 Add the eggs to the pan and turn in the paste to coat. Continue cooking, turning occasionally, for 4-5 minutes.

(Photograph, see page 126)

SCRAMBLED EGGS WITH ONION
(Piyaz Ekuri)

INGREDIENTS (Serves 2)
2 eggs, beaten
1 small onion, finely chopped
1 tsp chilli powder
2 curry leaves
salt
1-2 tbsp oil

1 Pound, grind, or blend in a liquidizer the onion, chilli powder and curry leaves, then mix with the beaten egg and ½ tsp salt.

2 Heat the oil in a pan, add the eggs and cook gently, stirring, until scrambled, for about 2 minutes. (The eggs will continue to cook after you have removed them from the heat, so be careful not to overcook.)

SPICED SCRAMBLED EGG *(Ekuri)*

INGREDIENTS (Serves 2)
2 eggs
1 small onion, finely chopped
1 green chilli, finely chopped
2 curry leaves
15g (½ oz) fresh ginger, finely grated
2 tbsp oil
salt

1 Beat the eggs well.

2 Stir together the onion, chilli, curry leaves and ginger.

3 Heat the oil in a pan, add the onion mixture and fry for 3 minutes, stirring.

4 Add the egg and cook gently, stirring, for about 2 minutes, until scrambled. (The egg will continue cooking after you take it from the heat, so be careful not to overcook.) Add salt to taste.

SCRAMBLED EGGS WITH MUSHROOMS AND PRAWNS *(Jhinga Kumban Ekuri)*

INGREDIENTS (Serves 2)
3 eggs, beaten
2 tbsp oil
1 small onion, finely chopped
75g (3oz) mushrooms, peeled and sliced
75g (3oz) peeled prawns
15g (½ oz) fresh ginger, finely grated
1 green chilli, finely chopped
75g (3oz) tomatoes, peeled and chopped
2 curry leaves
salt

1 Heat the oil in a pan, add the onion and fry until golden.

2 Add the mushrooms, prawns, ginger, green chilli, tomato and curry leaves and fry, stirring, for 5 minutes.

3 Add the egg with ½ tsp salt and cook gently, stirring, for about 3 minutes, to scramble. (The egg will continue to cook after you take it from the heat, so be careful not to overcook.)

(Photograph, see page 127)

ABOVE Whole Eggs Fried with Spice
(Unday Masala)
See page 124

ABOVE Scrambled Eggs with Mushrooms and Prawns
(Jhinga Kumban Ekuri)
See page 125

BREADS
Roti

Indian bread is flat, unleavened bread best eaten a few minutes after cooking. If you have an Indian grocer nearby, you will be able to buy chapathi flour or ata — unrefined flour which, in many homes in India, is ground by hand. Otherwise wheatmeal flour is a good substitute.

Breads are deep-fried or cooked on a hot tava or flat pan without any oil or fat, until they puff up and are speckled brown.

Stuffed bread (see page 129) can make a meal on its own with a vegetable curry and some chutney.

WHOLEWHEAT UNLEAVENED BREAD
(Chapathis)

INGREDIENTS (Serves 4-6)
225g (8oz) plain flour
½ tsp salt
boiling water

1 Sift the flour into a bowl with the salt and combine with as little boiling water as possible, about 3 tbsp, to make a dough that is soft but not sticky.

2 Form the dough into balls, roll and flatten them on a lightly floured pastry board to make small pancakes.

3 Heat a pan without fat or oil and cook the chapathi for about 2 minutes each side, until speckled and puffy.

NOTE
Chapathis can be half-cooked, for 1½ minutes each side, then frozen. The use of boiling water in this recipe ensures that the chapathis will be soft.

(Photograph, see page 131)

YOGHURT BREAD
(Puri Dahiwallah)

INGREDIENTS (Makes 12-14)
175-250g (6-8oz) plain flour
2-3 tbsp yoghurt
½ tsp salt
oil for frying

1 Sift the flour into a bowl, make a well in the middle, add the yoghurt and salt and combine with as little warm water as possible (about 3 tbsp) to make a dough that is soft but not sticky.

2 Pull off a small piece of dough and roll it into a ball on a lightly floured pastry board, then roll and flatten into a pancake. Repeat with the rest of the dough.

3 Heat about 2.5cm (1in) of oil in a pan, add the puri and fry for 2 minutes each side, until speckled and puffy.

(Photograph, see page 130)

DAL BREAD
(Dal Puri Roti)

INGREDIENTS (Serves 6-8)
175-250g (6-8oz) split yellow peas
4-6 cloves garlic, finely chopped
2 green chillies, finely chopped
1 tsp ground cumin
½ tsp turmeric
350g (12oz) plain flour
50g (2oz) butter or ghee, diced
2 tbsp oil
½ tsp baking powder
salt

1 Pick over the split peas, wash well and cook in about 850ml (1½ pt) water for 10-15 minutes, until the peas can be squashed under the back of a wooden spoon. Drain well.

2 Grind, pound or blend in a liquidizer the peas, garlic and green chilli. Mix the cumin and turmeric with 1 tsp water and blend into the puree, which should be dry rather than sloppy.

3 Sift the flour into a bowl, make a well in the middle and add the butter or ghee, oil, baking powder and ½ tsp salt. Combine the ingredients to make a dough, adding as little warm water as possible, about 3 tbsp. The dough should be soft but not sticky.

4 Pull off a small piece of dough and roll it into a ball on a lightly floured pastry board. Make a hollow in the ball and stuff in a spoonful of split pea mix. Stretch the dough to cover the stuffing, then roll and flatten the ball to make a small pancake. Repeat with the rest of the dough.

5 Heat a flat pan without any fat or oil. (You can buy a special chapathi pan — a tava — but a pancake pan will do.) Cook the puri in the hot pan for about 2 minutes each side, until speckled and puffy.

(Photograph, see page 130)

ABOVE Wholewheat Unleavened Bread
(Chapathis)
See page 128

ABOVE OPPOSITE Dal Bread
(Dal Puri Roti)
See page 129

BELOW OPPOSITE Yoghurt Bread
(Puri Dahiwallah)
See page 128

SAVOURY RICE

Chawal

Basmati is the best long-grained Indian rice. It is grown in the foothills of the Himalayas and can be aged for up to 15 years to mature its distinctive nutty flavour.

When you cook rice, the first thing to do is to pick it over. Measure out the required quantity and pour it onto a tray, then go through it removing any bits that are not rice. The next thing is to wash it in two or three changes of cold water and swirl it round until the water looks whitish in colour — this is the starch being washed off it. Drain and repeat until the water is clear. You may need to wash the rice more than three times.

If you have time, let the rice soak for at least 20 minutes before cooking and then drain very thoroughly. Rice should be cooked in 1½ times its volume of water. You can get the water quantity right by measuring both rice and water in a measuring jug.

Rice is often fried before it is boiled. You will need a heavy, flat-bottomed pot with a tightly fitting lid. Heat some oil in the pot and add the aromatics. Pour on the rice and cook gently, stirring, until it is translucent. This means that it has absorbed all the oil it can.

Add the water and bring to the boil, then turn the heat to very low, put on the tightly fitting lid and cook undisturbed for 20 minutes. After this time, stir the rice with a fork, then cover and continue to cook for about five more minutes, or until tender. The grains of rice should be separate.

The cooking process can be finished off in a slow oven to dry the rice if you prefer.

LEMON RICE
(Nimbowala Chawal)

INGREDIENTS (Serves 4)
300-350g (10-12oz) cooked basmati rice
2 tbsp lemon juice
¼ tsp asafoetida
½ tsp turmeric
salt
2 tbsp oil
½ tsp mustard seeds
1 tsp polished split black lentils (urid dal)
6 curry leaves
2 tbsp split gram, soaked in water for 20 minutes, then drained
15g (½ oz) fresh ginger, finely grated
1 green chilli, chopped

1 Mix the rice with the lemon juice, asafoetida, turmeric and salt to taste.

2 Heat the oil in a pan, add the mustard seeds, dal, curry leaves and split gram and fry until all the mustard seeds have popped.

3 Add the ginger, green chilli and rice and heat through, stirring, for about 5 minutes, until hot.

4 Add extra salt to taste.

(Photograph, see page 134)

TOMATO RICE
(Tamatar Chawal)

INGREDIENTS (Serves 4)
300-350g (10-12oz) cooked basmati rice
2 tbsp oil
½ tsp mustard seeds
2 tbsp split gram, soaked in water for 20 minutes, then drained
6 curry leaves
1 red chilli, cut into pieces
1 onion, chopped
15g (½ oz) fresh ginger, finely grated
2 cloves garlic, sliced
1 green chilli, chopped
350g (12oz) tomatoes, peeled and chopped
1 tsp sugar
1 tsp ghee
salt

1 Heat the oil in a pan, add the mustard seeds, split gram, curry leaves and red chilli and fry until all the mustard seeds have popped and the gram is golden brown.

2 Add the onion, ginger, garlic and green chilli and fry for 3-5 minutes, stirring.

3 Add the tomato and sugar and cook, mashing the tomato under the back of a wooden spoon to make a thick paste.

4 Stir in the rice and ghee and heat through, stirring, for about 5 minutes until hot. Add extra salt to taste.

(Photograph, see page 134)

RICE WITH YOGHURT
(Dahi Chawal)

INGREDIENTS (Serves 4)
300-350g (10-12oz) cooked basmati rice
225g (8oz) yoghurt
2 tbsp oil
2 tsp polished split black lentils (urid dal)
1 tsp mustard seeds
4-6 curry leaves
2 red or green chillies, chopped
salt

1 Mix the yoghurt into the rice, without mashing the grains.

2 Heat the oil in a pan, add the dal and fry until light brown.

3 Add the mustard seeds, curry leaves and chilli and fry until all the seeds have popped.

4 Stir the contents of the pan into the rice, mixing carefully, and add salt to taste.

(Photograph, see page 135)

ABOVE Lemon Rice
(Nimbowala Chawal)
See page 132

ABOVE Tomato Rice
(Tamatar Chawal)
See page 133

ABOVE Rice with Yoghurt
(Dahi Chawal)
See page 133

CHUTNEYS, SALADS & SNACKS

Accompaniments are served with every meal to give a greater balance of tastes and extra protein and vitamins. They are also eaten as snacks between meals. The streets of India are full of barrows selling appetizing delicacies — lentil patties, rice puffs, bread and chutney, roasted chickpeas — intended to inspire hunger in the passers-by, who can then eat them as they walk along.

There are several types of chutney. Some keep for months and are better after a period of maturing. Some keep for several days in a cool place, and others are made to be eaten straight away. Those cooked with vinegar, sugar and spices keep the longest. Pickles are marinated, rather than cooked. Fruit, vegetables, fish and even meat can be marinated and left to mature for long periods in spiced oils. Other chutneys are made from fresh herbs, such as coriander, and can be eaten immediately.

In Indian homes where dozens of different pickles were made, traditionally they would be left outside in the sun covered in muslin to mature by day and stored in a cool place with the lid on at night. Nowadays many of the chutneys are made in factories and they do not taste quite the same.

Pickles and chutneys can be spicy, sweet, tart, hot, sour, mild or aromatic. The more variety, the better. They are best served with plain foods such as rice and bread, or with lightly spiced dishes. They should not have to compete with the flavour of the dish they accompany, and they should certainly not overwhelm it.

A yoghurt relish called raita is often served to provide a cooling contrast to a hot spicy meal, and a refreshing salad of onion, lettuce, tomato and cucumber, dressed with lemon or lime, serves the same purpose.

COCONUT CHUTNEY *(Thankai Chatni)*

INGREDIENTS
100g (4oz) finely grated coconut
3 red chillies, chopped and seeded
50g (2oz) yoghurt
1 tbsp oil
½ tsp mustard seeds
4 curry leaves
salt

1 Grind, pound or blend in a liquidizer the coconut and 2 red chillies, then stir in the yoghurt.

2 Heat the oil, add the mustard seeds and fry until they have all popped, then add the remaining red chilli and the curry leaves and continue to fry for 2-3 minutes.

3 Add to the coconut mix with salt to taste.

(Photograph, see page 139)

TAMARIND CHUTNEY
(Amli Chatni)

INGREDIENTS
juice from 225g (8oz) seedless tamarind (see page 00)
1 tbsp coriander seeds
1 tsp peppercorns
½ tsp cumin seeds
½ tsp fenugreek seeds
1 tsp mustard seeds
½ tsp asafoetida
5 red chillies
2-3 tbsp oil
1 tsp polished split black lentils (urid dal)
1 tsp chana dal soaked for 20 minutes, then drained
6 curry leaves
25g (1oz) shelled peanuts
2 tbsp brown sugar
salt
1 tbsp sesame seeds
25-50g (1-2 oz) desiccated coconut

1 Heat a frying pan without any butter or oil and add the coriander, peppercorns, cumin, fenugreek, half the mustard seeds, half the asafoetida and 4 red chillies. Roast the spices for about 5 minutes, shaking the pan to prevent burning. Pound or grind the spices to a fine powder and set aside.

2 Heat the oil in a pan, add the remaining mustard seeds, the dal, split gram, curry leaves and remaining chilli, cut into 3 or 4 pieces, and fry until all the seeds have popped.

3 Add the peanuts and fry for a further 3 or 4 minutes, then add the tamarind juice, the roasted spice powder, sugar, ½ tsp salt and remaining asafoetida.

4 Heat another pan without fat or oil, roast the sesame seeds and coconut and add to the chutney. Stir well, adding extra salt to taste.

(Photograph, see page 138)

GREEN CORIANDER CHUTNEY
(Hari Daniya Chatni)

INGREDIENTS
leaves from 3-4 sprigs coriander
1 or 2 green chillies
15g (½ oz) fresh ginger, grated
salt
2 tbsp lemon juice
½ tsp sugar

1 Grind, pound or blend in a liquidizer the coriander leaves, green chilli, ginger and ½ tsp salt to make a thick paste.

2 Stir in the lemon juice and add sugar and extra salt to taste.

(Photograph, see page 138)

LEFT Tamarind Chutney
(Amli Chatni)
See page 137

BELOW Green Coriander Chutney
(Hari Daniya Chatni)
See page137

OPPOSITE Coconut Chutney
(Thankai Chatni)
See page 136

GREEN MANGO CHUTNEY
(Aam Chatni)

INGREDIENTS
225g (8oz) hard green mango
50g (2oz) finely grated coconut
1 red chilli or 1 tsp chilli powder
1 tsp mustard seeds
1 tbsp yoghurt
1 tbsp oil
4 curry leaves
salt

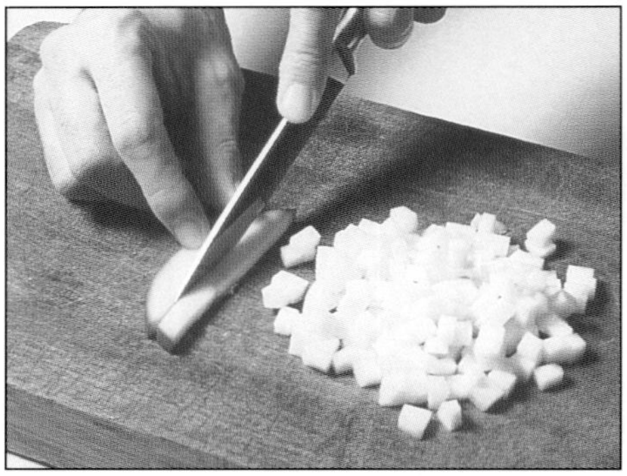

1 Chop the mango as finely as possible, with or without the skin.

2 Grind, pound or blend in a liquidizer the coconut, chilli and half the mustard seeds, add to the mango and stir in the yoghurt.

3 Heat the oil in a pan, add the remaining mustard seeds and the curry leaves and fry until all the seeds have popped, then stir into the chutney. Add salt to taste.

(Photograph, see page 142)

PEANUT SOYA SAUCE
(Seng Dana Chatni)

INGREDIENTS
100g (4oz) shelled peanuts, skinned
2 red chillies, cut into 3 or 4 pieces
½ tsp salt
2 tbsp soy sauce
1 tbsp lemon juice
1 tbsp brown sugar
2 tbsp oil

1 Pound, grind or blend in a liquidizer the first 6 ingredients.

2 Heat the oil in a pan, add the peanut mix, cook until it begins to bubble, then take off the heat and stir well.

(Photograph, see page 142)

BLACK LENTIL CHUTNEY
(Urid Dal Chatni)

INGREDIENTS
75-100g (3-4oz) polished split black lentils (urid dal)
1 or 2 red chillies
¼ tsp asafoetida
50g (2oz) finely grated coconut
juice from 25g (1oz) seedless tamarind (see page 19)
salt

1 Pick over the dal. Heat a pan without fat or oil, add the dal, 1 chilli and the asafoetida and cook, shaking the pan to prevent burning, until the dal is golden.

2 Pound the roasted spices together.

3 Grind, pound or blend in a liquidizer the coconut and tamarind with 1-2 tbsp water, then add the roasted spice powder and grind them together, adding a little more water if necessary.

4 Add salt to taste.

(Photograph, see page 142)

YOGHURT AND TOMATO RELISH
(Tamatar Raita)

INGREDIENTS
125g (5oz) yoghurt
100g (4oz) tomatoes, diced
1 small onion, finely chopped
leaves from 1 sprig of coriander
1 green chilli, finely chopped
15g (½ oz) fresh ginger, finely grated
½ tsp salt
½ tsp ground cumin, roasted without fat

1 Mix the tomato with the onion. You can reduce the strength of the onion by rinsing it in hot water, if preferred.

2 Mix the yoghurt with the remaining ingredients. Stir the dressing into the vegetables and add extra salt to taste.

(Photograph, see page 143)

ABOVE Green Mango Chutney
(Aam Chatni)
See page 140

ABOVE Black Lentil Chutney
(Urid Dal Chatni)
See page 141

ABOVE Peanut Soya Sauce
(Seng Dana Chatni)
See page140

ABOVE Yoghurt and Tomato Relish
(Tamatar Raita)
See page 141

SWEET TOMATO CHUTNEY
(Tamatar Ki Chatni)

INGREDIENTS
500g (1lb) tomatoes
50g (2oz) sugar
½ tsp ground cardamom seeds
3 cloves
½ tsp chilli powder
1 tbsp oil
½ tsp mustard seeds
1 tbsp white wine vinegar
salt
4 curry leaves

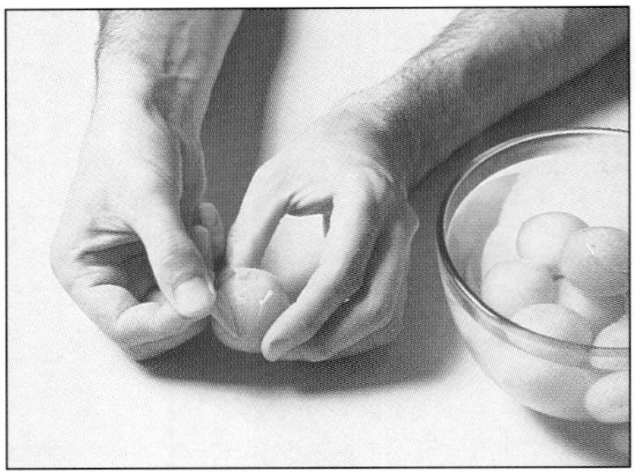

1 Immerse the tomatoes in a bowl of boiling water for about 2 minutes, until the skins split, drain them, allow to cool, peel and chop.

2 Bring 125ml (¼ pt) of water to the boil in a small pan, add the sugar and tomato and cook for 5 minutes, stirring.

3 Add the cardamom, cloves and chilli and continue cooking, mashing the tomato under the back of a wooden spoon to make a thick paste. Remove the pan from the heat.

4 Heat the oil, add the mustard seeds and fry until they have all popped, then add to the tomato.

5 Stir in the vinegar, add salt to taste and sprinkle over the curry leaves.

(Photograph, see page 146)

TOMATO SALAD
(Kachumbar)

INGREDIENTS (Serves 4)
500g (1lb) tomatoes, sliced
2 green chillies, finely sliced
2 tsp sugar
1 tbsp lemon juice
leaves from 1 or 2 springs of coriander
salt

1 Mix the tomato with the chilli.

2 Sprinkle with sugar, lemon juice and coriander leaves. Mix well and add salt to taste.

(Photograph, see page 146)

CABBAGE FRITTERS
(Gobi Pakoras)

INGREDIENTS (Serves 4)
100g (4oz) hard white cabbage, grated
100g (4oz) gram flour (besan)
1 small onion, finely sliced
2 green chillies, thinly sliced
15g (½ oz) fresh ginger, finely grated
4-6 curry leaves, chopped
1 tsp salt
½ tsp chilli powder
½ tsp garam masala (see page 17)
oil for deep frying

1 Mix the flour with 150ml (¼ pt) water to make a batter.

2 Add all the ingredients except the oil and stir well to coat.

3 Heat a quantity of oil for deep frying, add the cabbage in batter by the tablespoonful and fry until golden. Drain on absorbent kitchen paper.

4 Serve with chutney.

(Photograph, see page 147)

CHICKEN AND VEGETABLE SALAD *(Murghi aur Kachumbar)*

INGREDIENTS (Serves 4-6)
225g (8oz) cooked chicken, cut into manageable pieces
1 or 2 apples, cored and cut into segments
75g (3oz) white cabbage, shredded
2 tomatoes, cut into 8
1 green chilli, finely chopped
½ tsp ground pepper
¼ tsp ground nutmeg
salt
2 tbsp lemon juice
leaves from 1 or 2 sprigs coriander

1 Mix the chicken with the apple, cabbage, tomato and green chilli.

2 Sprinkle on the pepper, nutmeg and salt.

3 Squeeze over the lemon juice and toss the salad. Decorate with coriander leaves.

(Photograph, see page 147)

MELON WITH ORANGE JUICE *(Tarbuch aur Mosamki Ka Rus)*

INGREDIENTS (Serves 4)
1 honeydew melon
15g (½ oz) butter or ghee
½ tsp ground cumin
juice of 2 sweet oranges
1 tbsp lemon juice
2 tbsp sugar

1 Cut the melon into segments, remove the pith and seeds and cut the flesh from the skin. Cut into cubes.

2 Heat the butter or ghee in a pan, add the cumin and let it sizzle until the fragrance emerges.

3 Meanwhile, mix the orange and lemon juice with the sugar and 1 tbsp water.

4 Sprinkle the syrup on the melon, add the cumin and serve.

(Photograph, see page 146)

LEFT Sweet Tomato Chutney
(Tamatar Ki Chatni)
See page 144

ABOVE Tomato Salad
(Kachumbar)
See page 144

ABOVE Melon with Orange Juice
(Tarbuch aur Mosamki Ka Rus)
See page 145

ABOVE Chicken and Vegetable Salad
(Murghi aur Kachumbar)
See page 145

ABOVE Cabbage Fritters
(Gobi Pakoras)
See page 144

DESSERTS

Mithi

The simplest and one of the best ways of ending an Indian meal is with fresh fruit. In India this might be mangoes, guavas, jackfruit, pineapple, melon, cherries, oranges, apples or bananas. The Alphonso mango from Maharashtra in the west is considered the best of all. Most of these fruits should be readily available from any good grocery shop.

A mango is ripe if it gives a little when pressed. An unripe mango can be ripened at home in the airing cupboard, wrapped in paper. You can then chill it, peel it and serve it sliced, with or without cream. However, do not throw the stone away without nibbling off the rest of the flesh.

Desserts and sweetmeats are served on special occasions, such as weddings. Many of them are made with fruit, nuts, spices and milk. Coconut is a natural ingredient for a sweet dish, but more surprising is the imaginative use of vegetables for desserts. In this section you will find halvas made from pumpkin and beetroot. They look spectacular and taste absolutely delicious.

All the desserts here can be made quite easily at home, but there are many more elaborate Indian confections that are best left to the experts, who are nothing if not ingenious. Indian kulfi-wallahs (ice cream sellers), made ice cream long before there were freezers. They put the mixture into metal cones in a large churn made of clay, which was filled with pebbles, saltpetre and other natural substances and rocked until the ice cream froze.

PINEAPPLE PUDDING

(Ananas Pudding)

INGREDIENTS (Serves 2)
225g (8oz) canned pineapple chunks, drained
2 eggs
150ml (¼ pt) milk
100g (4oz) sugar
¼ tsp ground cinnamon
3 cloves

1 Arrange the pineapple pieces in a greased ovenproof dish.

2 Beat the eggs with the milk and sugar and pour over the pineapple, then sprinkle on the cinnamon and cloves.

3 Set the dish in a roasting tray of boiling water and cook in the oven at 160°C/325°F/Gas 3 for about 45 minutes until lightly set.

(Photograph, see page 150)

MANGO SOUFFLE
(Aam Pudding)

INGREDIENTS (Serves 4)
300ml (½pt) mango juice or 225g (8oz) mango pulp
4 eggs
2 tsp gelatine
2 tbsp granulated sugar
salt
2 tbsp caster sugar
½ tsp vanilla flavouring

1 Separate the eggs, putting the yolks into a mixing bowl.

2 In a small bowl, mix the gelatine with 3 tbsp water.

3 Beat the yolks well and mix thoroughly with the mango juice or pulp.

4 Stir in the granulated sugar, gelatine and ½ tsp salt.

5 Put the mixing bowl over a pan of boiling water, taking care that the bowl does not touch the water or the eggs will scramble. Beat the mixture for 10 minutes, then take off the heat.

6 Whisk the egg whites with ½ tsp salt and the caster sugar until stiff, then fold into the yolks, adding the vanilla flavouring.

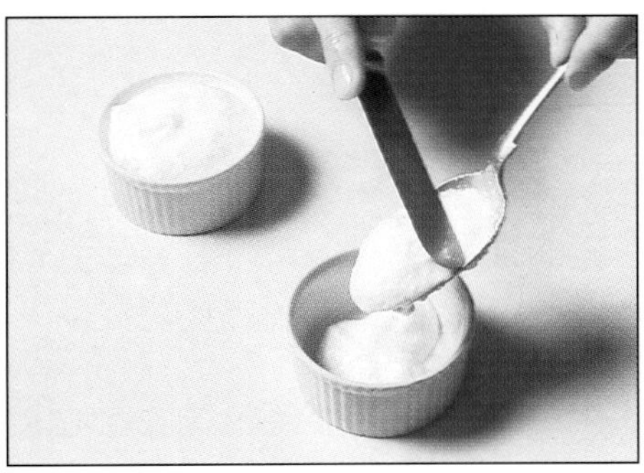

7 Divide the mixture between 4 small dishes and chill before serving.

(Photograph, see page 151)

BEETROOT HALVA
(Chukander Halva)

INGREDIENTS (Serves 4)
500g (1lb) beetroot
600ml (1 pt) milk
175g (6oz) sugar
100g (4oz) ghee
¼ tsp ground cardamom seeds
10 almonds

1 Scrape the skin from the beetroot, then grate coarsely.

2 Put the beetroot in a pan with the milk and sugar and cook gently for 30 minutes or more, stirring briskly, until all the milk has evaporated.

3 Add the ghee, cardamom and almonds and continue cooking, stirring all the time, until the mixture is heavy and sticky.

4 Spread the mixture in a greased dish with straight sides, in one layer about 5cm (2in) deep.

5 Leave for about 45 minutes to set, then cut into squares.

ABOVE Mango Soufflé
(Aam Pudding)
See page 149

OPPOSITE Pineapple Pudding
(Ananas Pudding)
See page 148

PUMPKIN HALVA
(Pethi Halva)

INGREDIENTS (Serves 4)
500g (1lb) pumpkin (preferably white)
600ml (1 pt) milk
125g (5oz) sugar
1 tsp rose water
100g (4oz) ghee
¼ tsp ground cardamom seeds
10-15 cashew nuts, halved

1 Scrape the seeds and stringy bits from the inside of the pumpkin, cut the flesh from the skin and chop into chunks.

2 Grate the pumpkin coarsely, put in a muslin cloth and squeeze out all the moisture.

3 Put the pumpkin in a pan with the milk, sugar and rose water and cook over a low heat for 30 minutes or more, stirring briskly, until all the milk has evaporated.

4 Stir in the ghee and continue cooking until it separates. Drain off any butter not absorbed by the pumpkin mixture.

5 Stir in the cardamom and cashew nuts and spread the mixture in a greased dish with straight sides, in one layer about 5cm (2in) deep.

6 Leave for about 45 minutes, until set, then cut into squares.

(Photograph, see page 154)

PLANTAIN JAGGERY
(Kela Gur)

INGREDIENTS (Serves 4)
4 ripe plantain, unpeeled
175g (6oz) jaggery (raw sugar; use brown sugar if jaggery is not available)

1 Cut the plantain into 5cm (2in) lengths, put in a pan and add just enough water to cover.

2 Add the jaggery and cook for 35–40 minutes, until all the water has evaporated.

3 Allow to cool, peel, then chill and serve cold.

(Photograph, see page 155)

STEAMED PLANTAIN CAKE
(Kela Cake)

INGREDIENTS (Serves 4)
3 or 4 ripe plantain, peeled and thinly sliced
175-250g (6-8oz) self-raising flour
1 tbsp melted ghee
50g (2oz) finely grated coconut
175g (6oz) brown sugar
½ tsp ground cardamom seeds

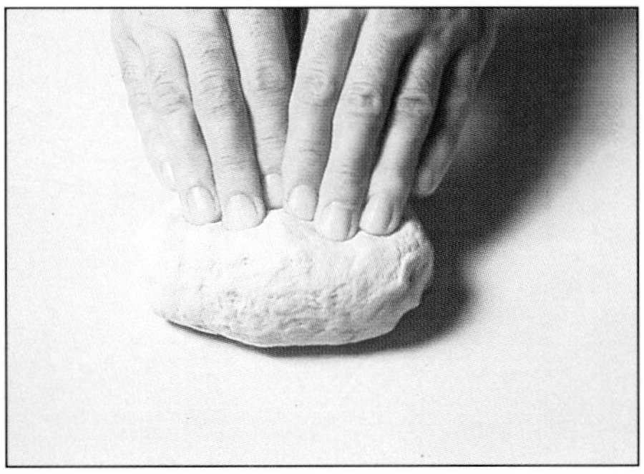

1 Sieve the flour into a bowl, make a well in the middle and pour in the melted ghee. Gradually adding as little warm water as possible (about 6 tbsp), work the ingredients into a smooth dough.

2 Mix the plantain with the remaining ingredients.

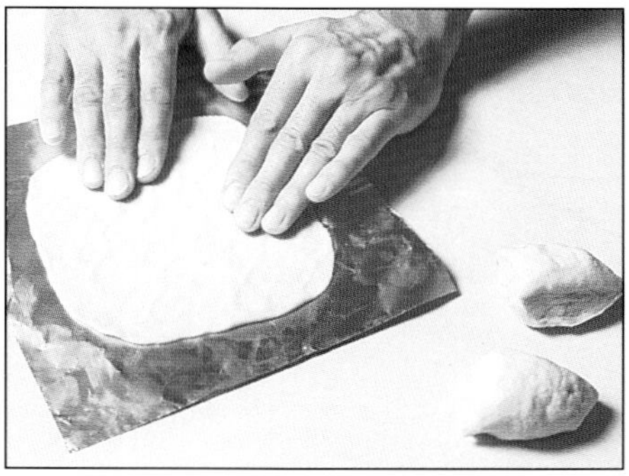

3 Cut kitchen foil into 4 × 23cm (9in) squares and divide the dough between them. With your finger or a spoon, dipped in water to prevent sticking, spread the dough out to within 2.5cm (1in) lengths of each side of the square.

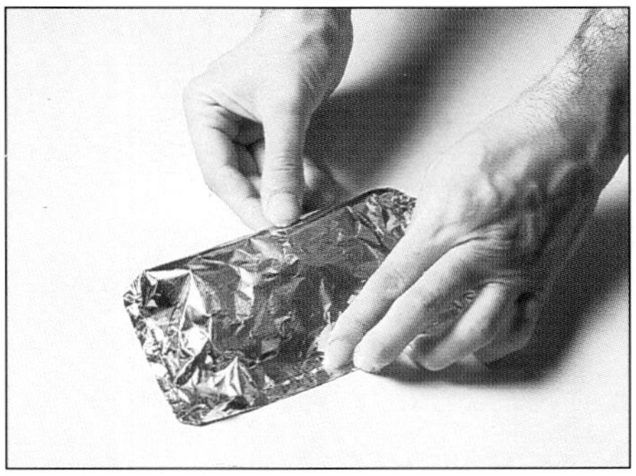

4 Divide the plantain mix between the sheets of dough and spread to cover.

5 Fold each foil sheet over in the middle and fold over the edges, pressing down well to seal.

6 Put the foil parcels in a steamer over a pan of boiling water and steam, covered, for 25-30 minutes, making sure that the foil does not touch the water.

(Photograph, see page 155)

ABOVE Pumpkin Halva
(Pethi Halva)
See page 152

ABOVE OPPOSITE Plantain Jaggery
(Kela Gur)
See page 153

BELOW OPPOSITE Steamed Plantain Cake
(Kela Cake)
See page 153

Glossary

Adrak Fresh ginger (see below).
Amchur Dried mango powder. Has a bittersweet flavour.
Amli Tamarind (see below).
Asafoetida A truffle-flavoured brown resin, available in powdered or lump form, and often used in cooking with beans. If you buy the lump form, crumble off a small piece and crush it between two sheets of paper.
Atta Wholewheat flour. Wheat is often ground at home in India and used to make unleavened flat breads.
Basmati rice The finest Indian long-grained rice, grown in the foothills of the Himalayas.
Besan Also known as gram flour, this is the flour made from chickpeas. It is used particularly in the south for making pancakes and steamed patties.
Biriyani A rice and vegetable, meat or seafood oven-cooked dish.
Cardamom Both black and green cardamoms are available, although the black ones are not often available. They are large and hairy. Use the green ones for the recipes in this book.
Chana dal A very versatile dried split pea. It looks like the ordinary yellow split pea, but is smaller with a sweeter, nuttier flavour. It can be cooked until soft for the dish called simply 'dal', or, as in southern India, it can be used as a spice.
Chawal Rice.
Chickpeas Also called gram or, in America, garbanzo beans. As chickpeas often demand hours of cooking before they become tender, it is often cheaper to buy the tinned variety unless you have an old-fashioned kitchen range.
Chillies Can be bought fresh, in which case they are normally green, or dried, in which case they are red. Chillies are very hot and should be handled with care and used according to taste.
Cinnamon Can be bought powdered or, better, in sticks. These sticks are the rolled bark of the cinnamon tree and have a warm spicy flavour.
Coconut Characteristic of the cooking of southern India. Buy a fresh coconut to extract the milk (see page 19) or use desiccated coconut to thicken sauces or garnish finished dishes. Desiccated coconut can be bought in most supermarkets and delicatessens.
Coriander Both the seeds and leaves of this plant are used. It can be grown as easily as parsley. The seeds are small and round, and are used either whole or ground. The leaves are bright green and have a strong bittersweet flavour.
Cumin seeds White or black, these seeds can be used whole or ground.
Curry leaves Can sometimes be bought fresh which is preferable to using them dried. Used extensively in the south of India, they are mainly added to food just before it is ready.
Dahi Yoghurt.
Dalchini Cinnamon (see above).
Dals Dried split peas, usually bought skinned.
Dhaniya Coriander (see above).
Elaichi Cardamon (see above).
Fenugreek seeds Chunky, tawny coloured seeds, often used roasted and ground. They have a bitter taste. Fenugreek leaves are a vegetable used like spinach, to which the plant is related.
Garam masala A mixture of spices ground together (see page 21), it is sprinkled on some dishes after they have been cooked.
Ghee Clarified butter. It can be made at home (see page 22) and does not need to be refrigerated.
Ginger Fresh ginger *(adrak)* is a fawn coloured rhizome. Ginger can also be bought powdered *(soondth)*.
Gosht Meat. Goat is the meat most often eaten in India.
Gram flour Made from chickpeas and also known as *besan.*
Haldi Turmeric (see below).
Halva A sweet dish.
Hara Green.
Hing Asafoetida (see above).
Jaggery Raw sugar, eaten as it is and used to flavour various dishes, even vegetable curries.
Jeera Cumin (see above).
Jingha Prawn or langoustine.
Kofta Meat or banana balls.
Kumban Mushroom.
Lassi A yogurt drink (see page 13).
Luong Cloves.
Machi Fish.
Masala Spices.
Masoor dal Skinned split red lentils.
Moong dal Skinned split mung beans.
Murghi Chicken.
Mustard oil A yellow oil made from mustard seeds that is pungent when raw and sweet when heated. Much used in Kashmir and Bengal.
Mustard seeds Small yellow or black seeds often popped in hot oil, when they have a nutty sweet flavour. When ground for mustard powder their character is quite different — hot and smarting.
Nariel Coconut (see above).
Neem Curry leaves (see above).
Papaya A fruit with good digestive properties.
Pilaf Fried rice dish.
Raita A cooling side dish made with yoghurt.
Roti Bread.
Sambar powder A southern Indian spice mix for vegetable curries (see page 23).
Soondth Powdered ginger (see above).
Tamarind The bean-like fruit of the tamarind tree, much used in southern Indian cooking.
Tava A flat cast-iron pan used for making bread.
Thali A large tray, often of wrought metal.
Toor dal A glossy dark yellow split pea.
Toran A style of cooking where the dish remains dry.
Urid dal Polished split black lentils, often used as a spice in southern India.
Vark Silver and gold leaf used to decorate food on special occasions. It is edible.
Vindaloo A highly spiced and hot curry, traditionally from Goa.

Index

Page numbers in *italics* refer to the illustrations